THE MAVERICK JOURNAL

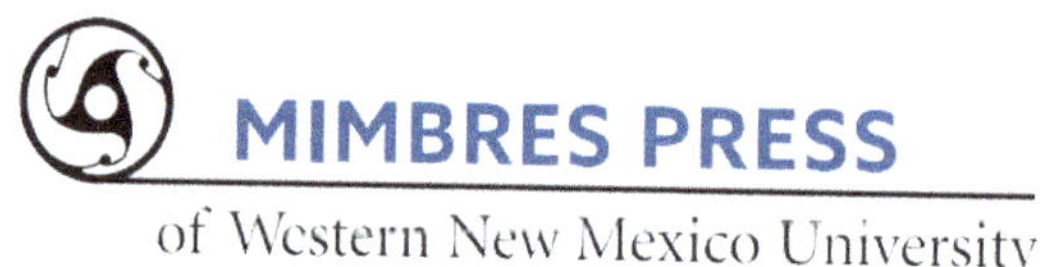

With this volume, we would like to honor Dr. Felipe de Ortega y Gasca, a founding father of Chicano literature and a cherished member of the WNMU (2007-2018) and Silver City community. Throughout his entire life, Dr. Ortega was devoted to uplifting other through his powerful writing, service in the United States Marine Corps and Air Force, and lifelong commitment to education and social justice. His legacy lives on in the countless lives he touched and voices he helped empower.

THE MAVERICK JOURNAL

UNDERGRADUATE ACADEMIC JOURNAL OF WESTERN NEW MEXICO UNIVERSITY

Special thanks to Professor Frankland, Marian Valle Angulo,

Dr. Oubre, Professor Brandt, Lee Allensworth, and Dr. Crocker

 No part of this book was generated using artificial intelligence tools. All content was conceived, written, and edited without the assistance of AI or automated writing technologies.

Cover Design by Anais Marie Orantez

Fourth Edition

Printed by Mimbres Press of Western New Mexico University

ISBN (paperback): 978-1-958870-29-7

THE MAVERICK VOL. 4

Western New Mexico University

TABLE OF CONTENTS

Essays

Fiction

Music composition/ Lyrics

Poetry

● = **Creative Writing**

◊ = **Editors features**

MEET THE EDITORS

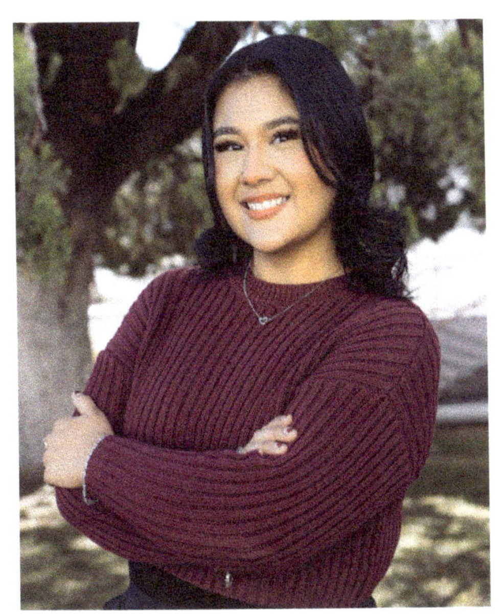

From the Pascua Yaqui Tribe reservation in Tucson, Arizona, Anais Marie Orantez is an aspiring journalist and storyteller, majoring in English with focuses in communications and music at Western New Mexico University. In her free time, she enjoys reading, writing poetry, and performing as a violinist and vocalist with Mariachi Plata de WNMU, which, in her opinion is the ultimate form of storytelling.

Laisha Vargas Garcia is a sophomore at Western New Mexico University. She was born and raised in Albuquerque, New Mexico. She is majoring in Business Management with a double minor in Music and Spanish. On campus, Laisha is not only a new member of The Maverick Journal editorial team, but she is also a violinist and vocalist for Mariachi Plata de WNMU, a senator in Student Government, and an activities director in M.E.Ch. A. As a proud hispanic/Mexican-American, Laisha is excited to bring her own flavor to the journal!

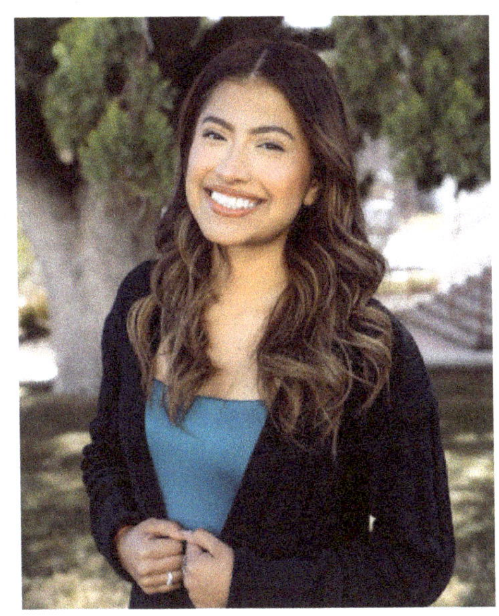

MEET THE EDITORS

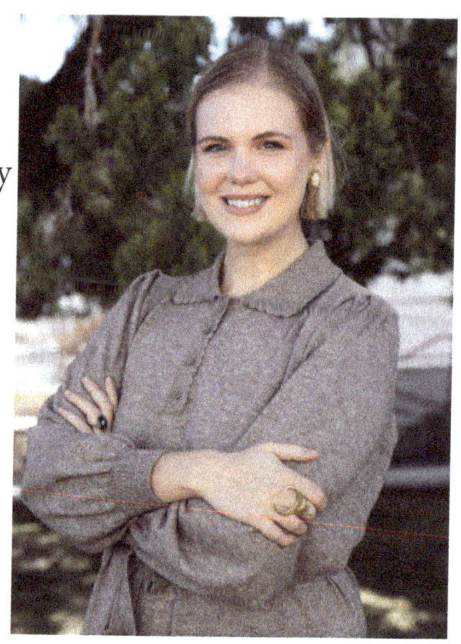

Arielle's life journey was by no means a direct route to Western New Mexico University. She was born and raised in a small town on the Jersey Shore, where she began her professional career as a makeup artist after graduating from The Paul Mitchell School. Upon her son turning three years of age, she decided that attending our beautiful university on the hill would be a natural progression in her journey. Arielle began her studies in the Fall Semester of 2024 and is now an English Major focusing on Literature and Composition.

A Letter from the Editor-in Chief

Dear Readers,

On behalf of the editorial team, we're pleased to welcome you to Volume 4 of the undergraduate-run academic journal of Mimbres Press and Western New Mexico University, The Maverick.

Looking back on this past year, it's clear that the need for love, compassion, and empathy has grown immensely, especially in a world that now feels unfamiliar. Within these pages, you'll find work from undergraduate Mustangs who speak to those values and reflect the heart of the WNMU student body.

As editor-in-chief, I'm truly honored to have led this volume alongside such a dedicated team. A very special thank you to Professor Frankland, Marian Valle Angulo, Bryant Chaffino, Laisha Vargas Garcia and Arielle Certosimo for helping to bring the vision for this edition to life. Without your help, and the handwork of our students, none of this would be possible.

Now, enough anticipation; let's venture into The Maverick!

In Lak'Ech,

Anais Marie Orantez

An Easter Morning

Maria Guzman

This is a story, one of many, from my childhood as the daughter of a drug dealer. Now that I am learning to write in English I want to tell stories of my life. I am not looking for sympathy.

My family consisted of Mami, Papi, my younger sister, and me. We lived in a two-room apartment in Juarez, Mexico, across a narrow dirt road from my father's mother. This tiny place was all Mami and Papi could afford. There were six two-room apartments made of concrete with little color except gray. These six apartments shared a shower, a vault toilet, and a water spigot. The spigot provided water for everyone's cooking, laundry, and drinking.

One Easter morning, I woke and saw two beautiful dresses, one white and one yellow, swinging from the clothesline in the shared courtyard. The dresses sparkled in the sun's rays. It was obvious Mami worked hard to make our dresses clean. My little sister found the dresses so enticing she immediately ran outside, stood on her tippy-toes, and tried to pull them off the clothesline. Mami, in her strong voice, told my sister, "NO." As soon as the dresses were dry, Mami carefully dressed us for Easter.

Traditionally, Hispanic families dress in their best for Easter Sunday church and spend more than they should. We dressed in our best, but instead of church, my parents would take my sister and me to Ascarate Park across the border in El Paso for the community egg hunt. My favorite part of Easter was hunting for colorful cascarón eggs (hollowed out eggs filled with confetti), then chasing Papi to break the eggs on his head and cover him in confetti. Chasing my six-foot father with cascarón eggs is one of my fondest memories.

When caught, he would lower his head to receive the honor of a cascarón from one of his little girls. I would giggle so hard my chubby dimples ached. I never got the opportunity to know if this was going to be one of those memorable Easters.

Papi took our hands and walked us through the hallway and across the dirt road to Grandma's house. My sister and I were excited to show Abuelita our lace dresses. Papi warned us to stay in the house and not get in trouble outside. Papi then left to visit with his cholo friends. As soon as Papi left, my sister, who never had trouble convincing me to break the rules, went outside, and I followed her without hesitation.

Everything Papi told us not to do, we did. Sister grabbed two buckets, and I dragged the water hose. We stood right by Abuelita's kitchen window and filled the buckets with water. I snatched two cups from the kitchen, and we went at it. Soon, our new, patent white leather shoes and ruffled socks were muddy and our dresses soaked. When Papi returned, we knew we were in deep trouble.

He dragged us into Abuelita's bathroom, tore off our clothes, and threw us in the running shower. He disappeared for a moment and came back with a broomstick in his hand. Papi started whipping us with the broomstick. I begged him to please stop. He did not. He beat me like a pinata while my sister hid behind me. I covered my face with my little hands while he struck my arms, legs, back, chest, thighs, and bottom.

When Abuelita could no longer bear to hear our little voices shrieking, she stopped the beating. Papi dropped his weapon and walked away. Abuelita wrapped her little ones in towels, and my towel filled with blood from my pompis. Mami, looking elegant in her black polka-dot dress and red high heels, entered Abuelita's house and did not look surprised to see her babies suffering and in tears.

Abuelita was not her usual calm self. She even called mom by her first name instead of 'ija. "Isela, what are we going to do about Maria's bottom?" Mom disappeared while I laid face down on Abueltia's lap. Mom returned as the sun was setting with a succulent plant. She and Abuelita sliced the plant into thin strips and placed them on my bottom. The plant was gooey, cold, and it burned. That night, I slept face down on Abuelita's couch. She comforted me all night and kept me safe.

I could have stayed home the next day with Abuelita, but sending me to pre-school in El Paso was part of the cover-up. Mom worked hard to ensure my school clothes covered the bruises. The teacher noticed I was in pain and asked me to roll up my sleeves. When she saw the bruises, she immediately sent me upstairs to her supervisor's office. The teacher and supervisor asked, "Who did this to you?" "What happened?" "Did somebody hurt you?" I was frightened that if I told the truth I would never see my father again, so I lied. I said no one hurt me; I just fell and hurt myself. They asked me many more times, but I stuck to my lie.

Finally, they stopped and called Mami to pick me up. She did not seem to have any embarrassment about what her husband did to her young child. She seemed more upset about having to leave work. As we walked home across the border, I held her hand and stared at the ground the entire time. For the entire two-hour journey, Mami didn't speak. When we arrived, Isela prepared dinner as if nothing had occurred. From the time mom picked me up, I was frightened I would be beaten more.

Until he was about 40, Papi was a violent man. Why he was violent is a mystery to me. Due to his minor hare lip, Papi was bullied by the neighborhood kids from the age of five. Maybe that made him mean and vicious. Papi now lives in an assisted living facility, and my daughters and I regularly visit him.

He is in his seventies, and it is hard to imagine such a frail man as ever violent or mean. I love my father unconditionally, even though he was incredibly abusive to me throughout my childhood. Until his death I will care for him, keep him safe, and clean his pompis. My daughters were stunned when they read these words as the Abuelito they know is kind and gentle. It was a challenge to write this story, but doing so was purifying. I am proud to share it.

The Thread of Failures and Successes

Tegen Uller

Then, a string of successes or failures follows,
each one different, yet the same at heart.
We rise, and fall, but still we move on,
chasing dreams that sometimes fall apart.
But in the stumbles, we find our way,
and in the wins, we learn to stay.
Success and failure, woven in the fray.

Give Me Your Money

Gabe Farley

give me your money
I can do so much more with it than you can
these dollars go much further when I have them in my world
I hold it out like a handful of cards
and fan off my heat-soaked skin
you have too much money already

the excess floats in your aura and in your memories of transaction
let me pull it out of the ether and your land of fantasy retirement
bank boxes and government servers
full of hidden numbers
the documents that have your name written on them

you were never safe from reality
I can turn it into something much more real
I plant the seeds of my change and grow the money trees
that offer shade and fruit to my community

to those born without the backing of your ancestors' psychopathy

to those whose reality rests entirely on their own shoulders

You sit on your pile of gold and hope that it brings you magic in your safety but

you are in stagnation

magic and stagnation do not mix, it is like water and oil

tell me how the waters of Tahiti and the Caribbean taste

tell me about the complex notes of oak and ash you can detect in your blood-wine tell me about

the dead magic of Chichen Itza as you walked through the trails in your sandals

I can make it real for you

I can give you the tangible benefits

Life sprouting from my fingertips

I build new worlds with my hands

you were never safe from death, my friend, so loosen up

And trust your funds to someone new

it's time to die a little

and to unclench your jaw full of dragon's teeth

let the rain smear the ink on the checks that you cash to yourself

let your write-offs evaporate in the burning sunlight

let loose your assets into the wind like kites on a storm

and drop your dividends deep in the heart of the earth

my own heart remains

fully resourced

even when these few numbers float in and out of my accounts regularly

teaching me about the tides

my imagination is on fire

and my hands create new movements constantly

finding new ways through the pain

maintaining my flexibility

because despite the crushing nature of this world that we have built up I still

believe in magic

so give me your money

and I will fold your 50 dollar bills into cranes of temporary liveliness I

will build nice benches for the homeless to sleep on

I will ignite new fires from your cash

and create the spaces for us to sit

in closeness and warmth

I will paint the streets with the greenery that you hesitantly let loose your grasp with

you were gonna die anyway

and when you do I will water your bones

with the rains of life and of magic

and give you reasons to free your clenched skeletal fists of their rigidity so

that you may return to the Earth fully

where there is an abundance of wealth mixed into the soil

and your spirit can remember

how to share again

WNMU HUMANITIES DEPARTMENT UNDER-GRADUATE CREATIVE WRITING CONTEST WINNERS 2024-2025

FEATURE I

What Doesn't Kill You Will Probably Kill You

Anais Marie Orantez

FIRST PLACE: PROSE

Laura woke up feeling... uncomfortable – to say the least. Charlie was damn near laying over her whole face, she was still in her jeans, and all the lights were on. The clock marked 7:34AM. She never made it to bed last night.

Sleeping was hard. All the time. Sleeping shouldn't be hard. Laura recalled trying to get up, but the couch pulled her in with the promise of safety. The lights were on, the TV was on, and Charlie was right in her lap. The light from the hallway shined brightly into the living area, but it did not whisper the same comfort as the voices that came through the screen. Another cup of coffee and some more TV and she would be fine. Besides, she was off from the restaurant tomorrow – an episode of *Ugly Betty* wouldn't hurt anyone.

One episode turned into four. *You need to go to your bed and sleep*, she thought while pouring the remaining coffee from the pot into her *Haunted Mansion* themed mug. Sleep sounded warm, but the sudden tingling in her right cheek made her snap out of sleepiness and into worry.

Pinching her cheeks to the point of fingerprints wasn't exactly Laura's favorite method of soothing herself, because it hurt. It hurt a lot. But how else was she supposed to stop feeling it? The ice cubes she would hold in her palms stopped working a while ago. Until she could feel the pain in her cheek – and as soon as it felt like the same pain on both sides – her breathing steadied and the tingling went away. By that time, Charlie had assumed his role of jumping on the counter and snuggling against Laura's chest, stretching his soft snout on her face, as if to help her feel the wet nose and whiskers accross her skin. Laura always felt particularly ashamed of these episodes, or whatever you would call them. As she wiped up the small spillage from the coffee, she thought about her room. It would be horrible to die of a stroke on her first night in her new room, on her new bed. So, she took her mug and planted herself back into her seat, Charlie following right after. The last Laura could remember was the clock reading 4:12AM and Netflix changing to the next season of Ugly Betty before she was transported back to the comfort of daytime.

Dragging herself to the shower, Laura blasted the latest episode of her favorite celebrity drama podcast to get ready for the day. She did not want to be alone, of course, but she also did not want to share the first embarrassing night in her apartment with anyone – so calling Carmen or Mom and Dad was out of the question.

As she lathered the shampoo in her hair and contemplated on what to do for the day, her phone chimed, interrupting the podcast and her thought spiral. Laura reached out of the shower to be met with her saving grace message:

7:47AM – anyone avail to work 8:30-6? Ray called out.

With ease, she smiled and replied:

7:48AM – i can!

Suddenly her worry about what to do for the rest of the day washed away. Laura rushed her shower and quickly got ready.

Foundation, concealer, blush, bronzer, powder, mascara, lashes, lipstick followed by a bun and a white button up shirt, paired with a knee length pencil skirt and black non-slip Mary Janes. Since it was getting cold, soon she would be able to change the skirt for pants. Her work outfit was nothing short of business casual, yet she was only a server. A server at one of the nicest restaurants in the city, yes, but a server, nonetheless. Sometimes she wished she didn't have to do the full face of makeup to serve – but only then would the high rolling customers complain, and she would be fired for not meeting the dress code.

At least, that's what Laura told herself.

The clock struck 8:10AM, Charlie was fed, and the next thought-spiral-invoking thing Laura had to do was drive to work, which was 10 minutes away. The walk to the car was the worst part of it all. Entering the stairwell to the parking garage of her apartment, Laura felt the rush of the unwanted enter her stream of thought.

What if I hit someone? The thought bombarded through the barricade surrounding her mind as she pictured the dozen bikers and joggers that might adorn the sidewalks for their morning movement.

Nuh uh. Not right now.

The floor slowly shook under Laura as she tried to keep walking, but the ugly thought stopped her right in her tracks again.

**

Right when she pulled out of the parking garage, she knew something was off. Laura tried to brake when exiting the apartment gates, but the brakes failed her, and she accelerated straight into the busy traffic.

Honking and hollering came from windows, telling her to "SLOW THE HELL DOWN!" but she couldn't slow the hell down because the fucking brakes weren't working.

The worst was coming. She knew it. Everything was moving in slow motion, but she knew the car was going miles and miles and miles over the speed limit. The park was coming near when she lost control of the wheel completely.

Thud after thud after thud after thud.

The car wouldn't stop.

Thud after thud after thud after thud.

The car wouldn't stop.

Thud.

Thud.

Thud.

Thud.

Thud.

Thud.

Thud.

Why won't it stop?

**

"Ma'am? Ma'am?"

Laura looked up to realize that she was still standing in the stairwell. Her palms were sweaty, and she had that nauseous feeling in her stomach she knew all too well. She must have been breathing hard too, because the stranger suddenly asked, "Are you okay?"

Laura was too embarrassed to say much, but she gave him a weak nod and replied, "Just some anxiety, thanks."

The stranger nodded and gave her a soft smile. "It'll get better." He walked away without leaving any room for Laura to feel uncomfortable, his soft brown locks bouncing above his ears as he trailed.

Laura looked down at her watch to see how long she had been out of it.

8:25AM.

Fuck.

Author's Bio:

From the Pascua Yaqui Tribe reservation in Tucson, Arizona, Anais Orantez is an aspiring journalist and storyteller, majoring in English with focuses in communications and music at Western New Mexico University. In her free time, she enjoys reading, writing poetry, and performing with Mariachi Plata de WNMU, which, in her opinion, is the ultimate form of storytelling.

A Lifetime of Change: Julie Dunleavy Reflects on 81 Years of Love, Art, and Resilience

Katie Ortiz y Pino

SECOND PLACE: PROSE

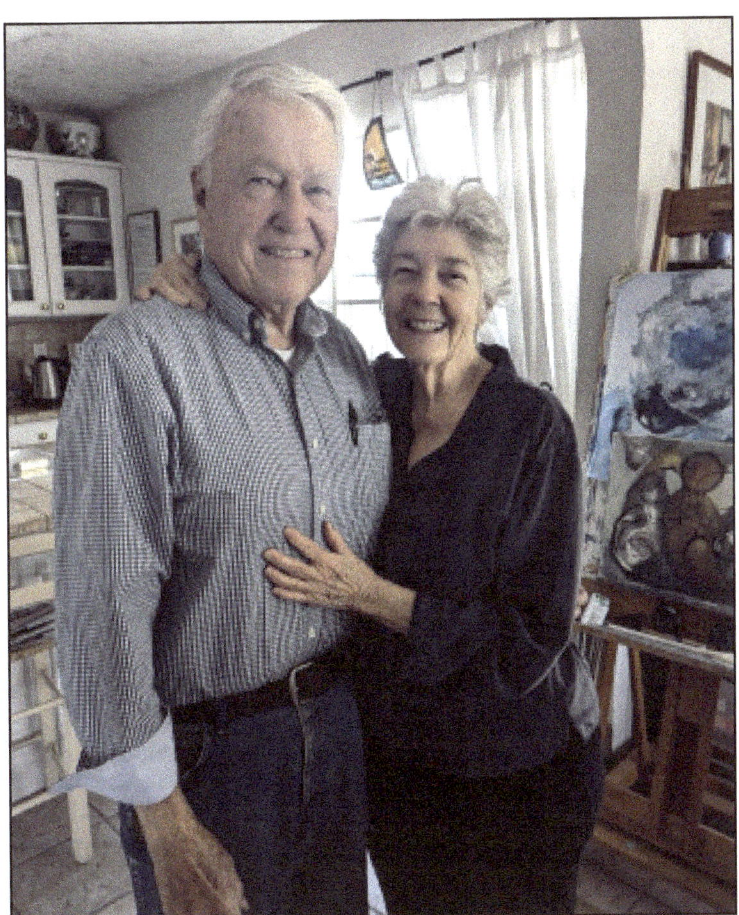

Joe Shepherd and Julie Dunleavy at their home in Albuquerque, New Mexico.

The small white stucco house in Albuquerque's Nob Hill District feels alive with color and light. Sunlight floods the dining room, bouncing off the wood floors that glisten beneath it. Crystals hang in the window, casting delicate rainbows across the room. At the center, a giant easel holds a half-finished painting with bold splashes of dark red, brown, and black that contrast with the serene warmth of the space.

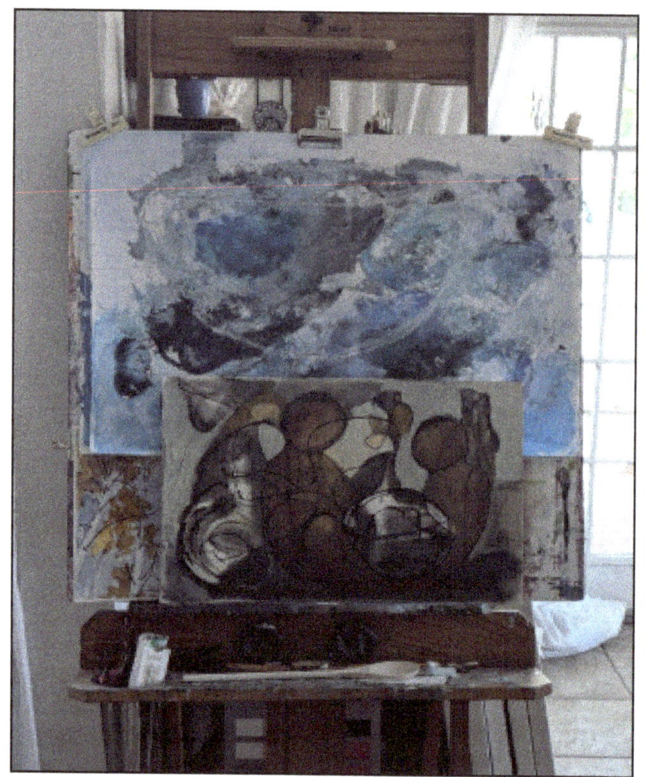

At 81, Julie Dunleavy has lived through eras of tremendous societal change. Standing at a petite 5'2" with a sturdy frame, her movements are slower after multiple knee surgeries. As she shuffles across the room, she groans softly but laughs it off. "Getting old isn't for the faint of heart," she jokes, flashing a warm smile that reveals her strength beneath her small stature.

Born in 1943 to a working-class family in Chicago, Julie's early years were shaped by the hustle and hardships of post-war America. When she was four, her family moved to Albuquerque, trading the tough streets of Chicago for the open fields of the South Valley. Her father, Philip Dunleavy Sr., was a civil rights attorney during a time when defending marginalized communities was often met with disdain. His passion for justice and equality led him to take on complex cases that others wouldn't touch. One case, in particular, broke his heart—he represented a Native American World War II hero who had been arrested multiple times for public intoxication. Despite her father's relentless efforts, he lost the case, a defeat that haunted him until his death.

"My dad was devastated," Julie recalls. "He couldn't understand how a man who bravely served his country was treated so poorly. He saw it as more than just a legal loss. It was a sign of how deeply rooted injustice was, especially for Native communities. It shook his faith in the system he had dedicated his life to."

Watching her father's heartbreak is where Julie's passion for social justice began to take shape. "I learned from him that fighting for what's right isn't always easy, but it's necessary."

Julie's childhood in the rural landscape of New Mexico was a mixture of simple joys and stark realities. "We had chickens, goats, and a big vegetable garden," she remembers. "It was a different world back then—simpler but not always easy." The rural life gave her a sense of freedom but also exposed her to the harsh realities of survival. One of her most vivid memories was watching her father slaughter chickens in their yard, a necessary task for feeding the family. The scene was both shocking and mesmerizing young Julie. The sight of the flapping wings and blood disturbed her, yet she couldn't look away.

"There was something so raw about it. The blood, the feathers—it was life and death right in front of me. That image stayed with me." However, as Julie grew up, she faced darker realities at home. Both of her parents struggled with alcoholism, deeply affecting the family dynamic. "It wasn't easy," she admits. "There were good days and bad days. But it was the only world I knew."

An excruciating memory from her childhood involves her mother's unpredictable temper. Julie played with her mother's makeup as a toddler, innocently spilling powder across the vanity.
When her mother discovered the mess, she flew into a rage, screaming at Julie before tying her to the bed for what felt like hours. "She lost her temper completely. I was so scared," Julie says quietly. "That kind of fear doesn't leave you."

After Julie's father passed away when she was 12 years old, her mother retreated even deeper into her alcoholism, leaving Julie and her younger brother, Phil, to fend for themselves. "It felt like we were raising ourselves," Julie recalls. The responsibility of holding the family together fell heavily on her young shoulders, forcing her to grow up far too quickly. Her mother's neglect only deepened the resentment Julie felt as she and Phil navigated their childhood without the care they desperately needed.

"We were just kids, but we had no choice but to take care of each other."

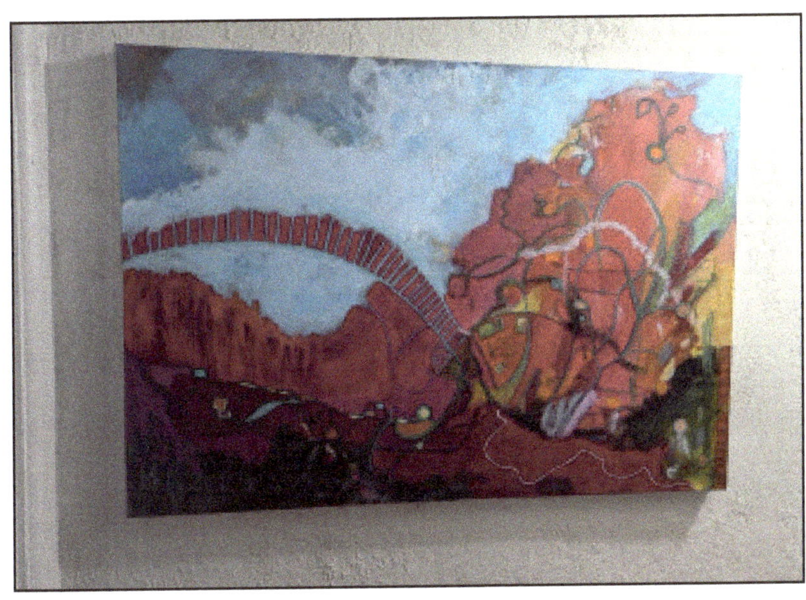

As Julie grew older, she found ways to navigate the complexities of her upbringing, turning to art as a source of solace. Painting became her refuge, a way to express emotions that words couldn't capture. Despite the challenges she faced, Julie found love—twice. Her marriages marked different chapters in a life entirely of reinvention, but it wasn't until she reconnected with Joe, a childhood friend, that she found her true partner.

Julie and Joe had been close as teenagers, and their friendship endured over the years. Julie quietly harbored feelings for him, but when Joe fell in love with Judy and married her, Julie put her emotions aside and was genuinely happy for him.

"It broke my heart a little," she admits, "but I was glad he found happiness with Judy."

Tragically, Judy passed away after a battle with terminal cancer, leaving Joe heartbroken. Years later, after life had taken them on different paths, Julie and Joe reconnected. Though they both carried sadness for Judy's loss, their friendship rekindled and blossomed into something more profound.

"We found joy again," Julie reflects. "It was a love built on years of shared history, and we both knew how precious life is." Together, they embraced this new chapter of companionship and love, grateful for the second chance at happiness. "We were just meant to be," Julie simply says. "He understood me like no one else."

Julie and Joe have traveled the world, collecting memories and making new friends along the way. As Julie and Joe have gotten older, the thrill of traveling remains, but it's become more challenging with age. While they once jetted across the world to explore far-flung destinations, they've recently adapted their adventures to suit their pace better. Instead of boarding planes for international trips, they travel across the country by bus, enjoying the journey just as much as the destination.

"It's harder to get around now, but we still try," Julie admits with a smile. "Taking the bus is slower, but we see much more of the countryside. We're still making memories, just in a different way. We've been everywhere—Ireland, Prague, Sedona. Just last week, we were in South Dakota for a bison roundup. It was incredible," she beams. "The people we met there, the stories we shared— it's the best part of travelling."

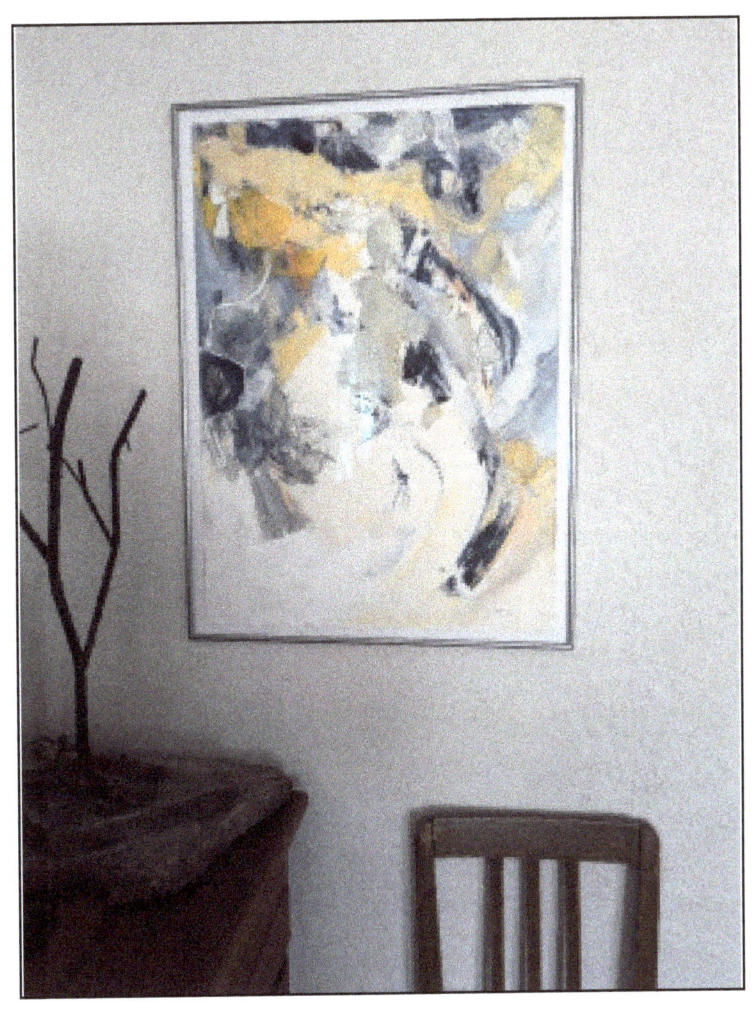

Julie's daughter, Miriam, reflects on the journey her mother has taken, especially the strength she displayed after a near-fatal car accident in 1985. In September that year, Julie's life was dramatically altered when another driver turned left into her path without yielding. The crash left Julie with severe injuries, including a serious closed-head injury that would have lasting effects on her life. The traumatic brain injury impacted her memory, and the recovery process was long and difficult. "I was a young adult when it happened," Miriam says. "It was terrifying. I remember seeing her in the hospital, hooked up to machines, and thinking she might not make it. But somehow, she found her way back—and then some."

Miriam witnessed a profound transformation in her mother as Julie immersed herself in painting during her recovery. What began as a therapeutic outlet soon became a deep passion that allowed Julie to express herself in ways words couldn't. As the years passed, Miriam watched her mother's skills develop and flourish, with each new painting reflecting layers of emotion, growth, and healing.

"Mom came alive through her art," she says. "It wasn't just a hobby—it became part of her identity. Her paintings are these amazing, emotional landscapes. You can see all of her in them."

Julie's later years have been filled with love, adventure, and creativity. Thanks to her dedication to learning and improving, her art has flourished. She's taken art classes at the University of New Mexico, sharing space with younger students, and continued her education through online courses, constantly seeking new techniques and inspiration.

"Every day is a chance to get better," she says. "I'm never done learning. There's always a new way to see the world, a new way to express it through art." This commitment to growth has shaped her work into something deeply personal, constantly evolving, just like her life. "I've been through a lot," she says.

"But I'm lucky. I have Joe, my children and grandchildren, my art, and I've lived more than I ever thought possible."

Looking ahead, Julie reflects on society's progress during her lifetime, particularly in civil rights, women's rights, and LGBTQ+ acceptance. "We've come a long way from where we were," she says. "There was a time when people didn't speak out, didn't stand up for what was right. Now, there's more awareness, more voices being heard." But she's also concerned about the fragility of that progress.

"It feels like sometimes we're at risk of slipping backward, especially when it comes to how we treat marginalized and minority groups," she continues. "There's still so much work to do— systemic racism, inequality, and discrimination haven't gone away, and we have to keep pushing forward or risk losing what we've fought so hard to achieve." Julie knows that without vigilance and continued advocacy, society could regress.

"Progress isn't guaranteed," she warns. "It's something we have to protect and build on. I'd love to live long enough to see the first woman president," she says with a grin. "We've come so far, but there's still more to do."

At 81, Julie Dunleavy's life is a testament to resilience, love, and the power of art to heal. Surrounded by the color and light she's created, her story is one of triumph—proof that even through hardship, beauty prevails.

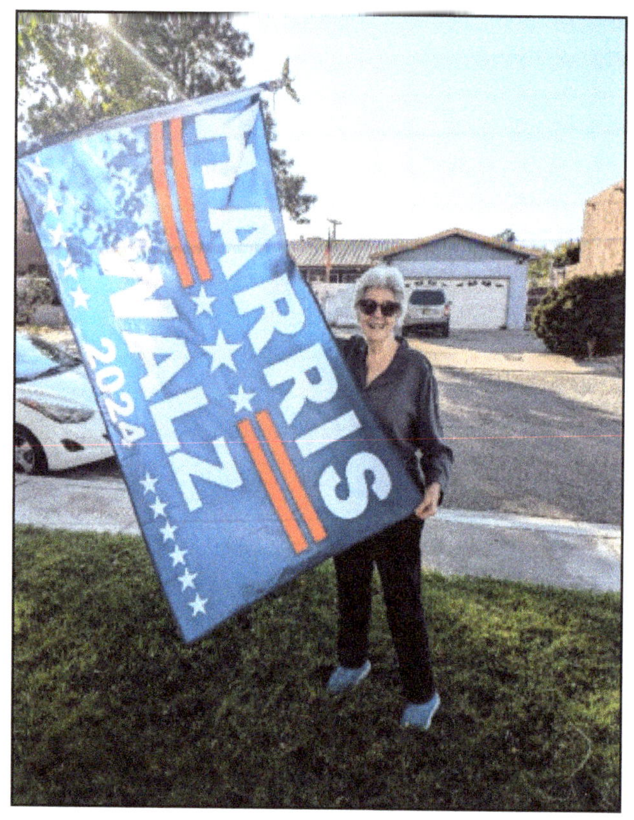

Author Bio:

Katie Ortiz y Pino, a dedicated mother and wife, is pursuing a degree in Social Work at Western New Mexico University. Originally from Albuquerque, New Mexico, she also lived in Queen Creek, Arizona, and Portland, Oregon, adding to her diverse life experiences. Katie is a dog mom to three beloved pets: Olive, a 16-year-old mixed breed. Cookie, an 11-year-old Australian Shepherd, and Chip, a two-year-old Siberian Husky mix, the baby of the family.

Katie's journey has been shaped by her experiences with addiction and long-term recovery. Having spent much of her adult life battling addiction, Katie has emerged with a profound understanding of the challenges others may face. Her passion lies in helping those who need extra support, drawing from her experiences to guide and empower others as they navigate their paths to recovery.

In her free time, Katie enjoys expressing creativity through art projects. Katie won the NM State Science Fair in Behavioral Sciences and the NM Metro Art Show in high school. Her main priority remains raising her children, ensuring they are supported in every way. Katie is eager to channel her experiences and education into a career that makes a meaningful difference in the lives of others.

Year of the Dragon

Arielle Certosimo

FIRST PLACE: POETRY

Fire

Creator of Dragons

Feed me

Desires

Pines

Curling and clawing

Like lobsters in a boiling pot

The roar

Primal

Elegant

Element

Journey through darkness

Gathering limbs of Juniper

Instinct initiated

Embers embracing amber golden hope

Always living

Always dying

Just like me

Pulsing and sparkling

Just like me

The Dragon rears it's gorgeous head

Just in time for a New Year

Author Bio:

Arielle is a domestic goddess residing in Silver City, New Mexico. A mom, a wife, a student of life and a creative without edges, she loves exploring both the known and unknown realms.

My Unearthly Adolescence

Natalee Drissell

SECOND PLACE: POETRY

In the folds of the fabric of reality I carved my initials with pieces of shattered starlight;
The forms of existence hold traces of my teenage graphite.
In my desperation I strove to drink the creamy light of the galaxy,
but I was too afraid of its endless milky waves.
As growth pains agonized my body, I cried out in sonic waves,
waves that sounded off in distant solar systems ten thousand years away.
And I learned the hard way that what you shove down the gaping twilight jaws of a black hole
is
gone
for
good.

Author Bio:

Natalee Drissell is a sophomore from Silver City majoring in Expressive Art and minoring in Creative Writing. When not writing or creating art, Natalee can be found curled up with a Tolkien novel or wandering through the local wilderness looking for secret hideaways.

Essay 2: Narrative and Context of the Place

Latasha Valdez

Department of English: Western New Mexico University

ENG 1120: Composition II

Up in the northwest of New Mexico lies a small village called Cañones. Unlike other small townsites or villages, it is the perfect mixture of silence and peace, as there is no cell service, smog, or light pollution. The only civilization with stores, gas stations, and schools is about twenty miles in one direction and about an hour in the other. What makes this place peaceful for me is the moment I drive off the paved road, and I am met with nothing but a dirt road and fresh air. I begin to yearn for comfort and security that can only be handed to me by nature. The moment I enter this small village, the first thing I see is a cemetery to my right, followed by another dirt road extending just over the hill into what I can only describe as an extension of wanderlust mixed with a desire to dig deeper.

By taking this road, I feel as if I'm stepping into another world—one that frees me from the shackles of the reality I've been trapped in. As I take turns and bounce around from the bumps the road has created, my only thought is what prompted me to take this new road and what my next destination will be at the end of it. For me, that destination is my grandparents' ranch. Since I was a child, as much as I loved spending every moment with them, I always craved and wanted more time to soak myself in the sun and the creek that flows through the very property that made me appreciate nature.

With tall, beautiful trees that dance with the wind, and the sound of the creek that cuts straight through the land sings in harmony, along with the mixture of a shiver from the shade of the mountain and warmth from the fire raised in the sky was always the perfect description of how I wanted to be in sync with who I am and what I want to grow up to be. The importance of this land symbolized that no matter how far away I am or how much I have grown, it will still look the same as if time is frozen in place, and I will always have a sense of belonging the moment I step back into the past. I will always hold tightly to the memories I have made with my family, knowing that one day, they will pass it down to my sister and me, as it has become our family heirloom. Not only is it important to me, it is also special to me in the way that it gave me the freedom to see the world free of troubles and worries. I did not think of it this way at the time because you have no troubles or worries as a child. However, now that I am older and have experienced the real world, the ranch is the only place I can lose and find myself in the same breath. On top of all this, it is the history that has carved and made its mark on the land that will forever bind me to the place I will always call home.

My first historical thought about the land was if there were any legends or Native American history, and to my surprise, there were. Sitting at the top of the canyon, between my grandparents' house and their ranch, lies the ruins of Tsiping (Tsi-p 'in-owinge), also known as the "Village of Flaking Stone Mountain." According to the New Mexico Bureau of Geology and Mineral Resources (2023), the village was occupied sometime around 1200 AD-1325 AD. My grandparents used to tell me stories about how the Native Americans occupied the land, and now, their spirits stay on top of the very canyon, watching over and blessing the land we now inhabit. My grandparents have hiked to see these ruins, and the thing they had to say about was "how beautiful" it was to see it for themselves.

My grandmother has explicitly visited the ruins three times, and she recalls finding broken pieces of pottery and arrowheads each time. My grandfather, however, has recalled finding broken pottery pieces scattered in the valley below near our family ranch, but they always made sure to leave them undisturbed as they have become part of the land. Unfortunately, the ruins are a part of the Sante Fe National Forest and can only be visited via permit, but knowing this information, it is safe to say that they will always be protected.

Fast forward to today; the ranch has been in our family for three generations since 1942 and currently covers about twelve acres. After speaking with my grandfather, I learned that the land was gifted to him by his father in 1991. When asked if his father (my great-grandfather) inherited or bought the land, half was gifted by his uncle in 1952, and the other half was bought between $1,100 and $1,500 a few years later. Since then, my great-grandfather and grandfather have used the land strictly for farming and grazing cattle. The only issue with farming and grazing cattle is the wildlife we live with in the canyon, such as deer, elk, bears, and mountain lions. Still, it makes the lifestyle worth it. Learning more about the history of my family's ranch makes me appreciate what we have and how long it's been in our family. The next time I return to the place I call home, I will see it for what it truly is: a forever home. I will also have a deeper understanding of the lengths my grandfather has gone to keep it beautiful and ensure that my sister and I will always have a piece of him and our ancestors.

After conducting research on the land and my family, more questions remain. What prompted the people of Tsiping to disappear? I wonder if someone or something forced them out or if the tribe was hit by disease. When I see ruins in general, it always strikes me how these homes can be abandoned without a trace of where they went. Maybe they did leave traces, and the earth washed it away as a form of protection, and maybe they never did. The more I think about ruins, the more curiosity I have. Are there more Native American ruins near my grandparents' ranch? I have learned that if you want to be a part of the land, you have to know the land. I know that with more research, I will discover many ruins and learn how long they have been there and who they belonged to. Speaking of researching how long ruins have been around, I begin to speculate if the ranch has been in my family longer than what my grandparents have documented. My grandmother has titles dating back to 1942, but how my family inherited the ranch is unclear. Lastly, how did my ancestors know this location could be used for farming and grazing? The location sits in a valley along the northwestern part of the Santa Fe National 9 Forest. Without traveling, you would have to zoom in on a map to see the line of ranches within this valley. I wonder if this relates to my previous speculation of my family's land inheritance. If so, was this information passed down with it or taught to the generations that follow?

During the time I was learning more about what makes my family ranch special and important to me, I also realized that even when I feel like I've known something my entire life, there are still more details and information I have yet to grasp. Having this extra knowledge makes me want to cherish it even more. It makes me feel more connected to it—both physically and emotionally. I also learned that research is essential, especially when I feel deeply about something because it can alter my perception and help me become more in tune with the world. This experience of discovering more about my family lineage and the land tied to it was informative, emotional, and heart-warming. It helped me understand that there is still more to uncover and discover no matter how close I come to the truth.

Research Questions:

1. What was the ranch used for then and now?

Answered by my grandparents: farming and grazing cattle.

2. Was the land purchased or gifted? If purchased, how much was it?

Answered by my grandparents: It was my great-uncles in 1942 who then gifted half to my great-grandfather in 1952 (he purchased the other half for $1,100-1,500 years later), and then gifted to my grandfather in 1991. The ranch is currently 12.22 acres.

3. Are there any legends or Native American history associated with the land?

Tour: Tsiping. (2023). New Mexico Bureau of Geology & Mineral Resources. https://geoinfo.nmt.edu/tour/landmarks/tsiping/home.html

4. How long has the ranch been in our familial bloodline?

Answered by my grandparents: three generations.

5. What type of wildlife inhabits the land?

Answered by my grandparents: elk, deer, mountain lions, bears, turkeys, cows, horses, etc.

6. Have there been any artifacts discovered, such as arrowheads, pottery, or petroglyphs?

Answered by my grandparents: within the ruins and in the canyon, never on the ranch itself, and left all artifacts untouched. My grandmother stated she hiked three times to the ruins, twice on foot and once on horseback, starting in the summer of 1974.

Warmer At All

Natalie Ann Prieto

I've got a deck of tarot, a pendant and cross
Dozens of candles that glow on the
wall I pick through my dreams
I search the bathroom stalls
I just want to know You
Am I getting warmer at all?

I go to Mass weekly and hear others pray I
sing all the sermons and join with voice raised
You and Your Family still only look down
And I to your pictures on the wall
I just want to know You
Am I getting closer at all?

I fill bottles with sacred water

I chant till midnight and speak with the stars

I've sat in dead silence in trees and hospitals

I have my rosary with white plastic beads

I bought at the mall

I just want to know You

Am I getting through at all?

I feel You around me

in the air that I breathe

I know we don't talk

I'd like to hear You speak

I just want to know You

I hope You know me

Am I getting warmer at all?

Our Spaces, Our Hearts: Rebuilding Our Public

Gabe Farley

Western New Mexico University

ENGL-1120: Composition 2

Every morning, I wake up and prepare for the day by pouring my coffee and leaving my apartment. I get in my car; I drive to work. I navigate through the stress of the road, where the base interaction I have with other people is through the windshield of my vehicle and the sounds of my podcasts; I am alone. I arrive at my workplace, and I activate my professional mode. I suppress myself and my needs for connection and sharing with my colleagues for the sake of efficiency and cultural norms within the work environment. I work through my day, uncertain how to communicate with those closest to me, and realize they remain strangers in many ways. As the day and the work go on, I will eventually leave with some sense of estranged satisfaction around my work and the money I made. It makes it all feel worth the stress of that internal disconnection. I drive away and head towards my apartment once again and reenter the shared realm of traffic-based interactions behind the glass and metal of my car, while others around me do the same. I get home, and it is evening. I find my routine way to cope with the day's stresses by sitting and putting on a TV show or a video game that temporarily satisfies my needs for connection. I go to sleep, wake up, and do it all again. My therapist tells me I have such debilitating anxiety that it is approaching obsessive-compulsive disorder, and my stress is causing me to have panic attacks regularly. What am I doing wrong? What is absent in my life? I was told that I am doing everything correctly and living as I am supposed to be. In many ways, this society tells me this is normal and a good life. Yet, I can feel that void that persists despite continuing along this path. Needs are not being met: my friends, my community, my family, my relationships. I sense that the problem is my connection with people, and ultimately, my environment, socially and physically. I am lonely, and I think everyone else is too. But where did everyone go, and why is it so difficult to maintain a healthy balance? Why are these environments causing enormous stress, and how might we live differently? Silver City, New Mexico, the town I call home, is in the scenic southwest corner of the state. It can be a haven and has offered me much in the realm of community; it has kind people, lovely natural areas with walking trails, a sense of nature, a cute little downtown area, and is not extremely busy or overcrowded. I am glad that I continue to live here, and yet, there's this sense of incompleteness I experience daily. This town lacks essential pieces of infrastructure crucial for creating a thoroughly cohesive living environment conducive to the health and well-being of its residents, and it appears that it is much worse in many other parts of this country. I've realized that what this town lacks, alongside many other population centers across the country, are stable, functional, and comfortable public spaces; spaces that assist in decreasing feelings of isolation and increasing a sense of connectedness. Where did our public places go, and how can we return them? Towns and cities need public squares, plazas, natural spaces, and a sense of cohesion to tie it all together for the benefit of their residents. We need spaces that make it feel good to exist and to be alive, and most importantly, allow us to connect with the other people who live here. Silver City and the adjacent populated areas of Grant County should contain areas developed for large- scale public access, designed to embrace community, sharing, and a sense of conviviality and liveliness. We should create and develop public places around the town that everyone can access to encourage better human interactions and community connections. The results of investment into such projects have the potential to increase the base level of well-being and connectedness with the many people of this town, decreasing feelings of isolation, depression, and anxiety. To exist within a community, it is essential to have consistent and easy access to the people and places that form that community. Public spaces, or 'The Commons', hold the key to getting people to come together, and we need spaces that fit an extensive range of behaviors and uses to foster a liveliness and emotional connectedness between community members and the natural environment. Public spaces belong to everyone—they are our common ground, where communities connect. In turbulent times like these, when unprecedented isolation and global anxieties threaten to pull us apart, these shared places remind us how to come together. To design public spaces that genuinely serve our needs and well-being, we must first understand how we arrived at our current reality, where authentic public spaces have become increasingly scarce or inaccessible. In much of the U.S., public spaces have been gradually dismantled. Let's examine that dismantling more closely, as much of it was carried out by the automotive industry. "Before the 1950s and 1960s…the US had dense, European-style cities" (Allen, 2021) "Communities had walkable neighborhoods with wide sidewalks, narrow tree-lined streets and robust streetcar networks." These cityscapes, built across the continental United States, contained many of what we would today call public and social spaces. These spaces were baked into the framework of society, and many people used them. Our cities and towns "had large central squares that served as meeting places, open markets for buying and selling goods, and parade grounds for special occasions" (Melosi) . People spent time outside, walking, chatting, and connecting on some level regularly in these city spaces. The popularization of the automobile in post-WW2 America and a large-scale economic push towards car-centric infrastructure caused all that to change. Over time, (Allen, 2021), thus destroying many public spaces and erasing entire historic neighborhoods, especially in marginalized or impoverished communities. Nowadays, in many parts of the country, the urban infrastructure of cities revolves around the car as the primary method of travel and human interaction, cutting off natural socialization among people and resulting in our environments being dominated by asphalt and concrete. This means that now "the experience of walking in these cities is at best unpleasant and inconvenient, and at worst nearly impossible and dangerous" (Allen, 2021). Urban environments that were once pleasant and navigable are now stressful, hostile, and dehumanized.

That hostility extends beyond the expansive car-centric infrastructure. Hostility is increasingly becoming a deliberate component of design and architecture in many public settings. The design principles behind 'hostile architecture', also known as defensive design, are simple; it is a type of architectural design, found primarily in public places, "where the built environment purposefully guides and restricts [human] behavior" (Wiseman, 2024). Hostile architecture can be a method used consciously and with deliberate intent to limit occupation, or it can be an unconscious side effect of bad design. Examples of deliberate defensive design can include park benches imbued with a particular discomfort, which make lying down impossible or painful. Another example would be concrete or metal spikes mounted on the ground, either near businesses, parks, or under bridges and highway overpasses. Both these examples are designed specifically to deter mainly homeless people from sleeping or loitering, "but, increasingly, it has the added effect of making a city less comfortable for everyone else" (Wiseman, 2024). Examples of when hostile architecture may be less-than overtly malicious "can be as subtle as simply not providing a place to sit" (Hu, 2019) or by not protecting a seating area from the sun in summertime. It can also look like virtually any grocery store's parking lot. As a simple example, parking lots are generally stressful, ugly black asphalt fields, and conveniently, can help to pull the customer from the chaos of all the cars coming and going, from the lot and into the safety and luxury of the attached store. Designs like these heavily influence our decisions to spend time in an area or engage with the local people and infrastructure. Hostile architecture can do a great job at making you subconsciously desire not to participate in public outings, or express interest in your community. Design can kill potential for connection just as easily as fostering it. Another way that public spaces have suffered is the implementation and takeover of privately-owned public spaces as the spiritual successors to actual public spaces, that is, actual publicly-owned spaces. Privately- owned public spaces, or POPs, are places that, on some level, a person is allowed to visit and spend time, think: "open-air squares, gardens and parks that look public but are not" (Garrett, 2015). While these spaces may feel open and available on one level, they are often surveilled and guarded by the property owners and can act as a huge limiting factor on the types of actions and behaviors that can occur, and can silently enforce minimal social interaction "When space is controlled… we tend to police ourselves, to monitor our behavior and to limit our interactions, especially after embarrassing confrontations with security" (Garrett, 2015). This can be considered an entirely new subclass of hostility. Have you ever seen one of those little green spaces attached to a bank, an office building, or a parking lot? Have you ever wanted to sit in that grass and enjoy the shade for a while, but you knew that you were not allowed to on some level, and that if you were to spend significant time there, an employee, security personnel, or the police would eventually arrive and instruct you to leave? It might look like a nice park, but it is a privately controlled space. POPs operate under the same modality, but on a different scale and with slightly different rules. On a certain level, we understand the subtle policing that occurs in these places because they are not quite as free as we'd like them to be. These POPs can act as "dead public spaces" because "the essence of conviviality, spontaneity, encounter, and yes, that little sprinkle of chaos has been stripped out" (Garrett, 2015). Yes, to benefit from a real public space, we must withstand a certain amount of unpredictability, as an aspect of conviviality—liveliness. The rigidity in such spaces makes the base interaction all the more stressful. It can be very beneficial for our internal systems not to have our social worlds so highly controlled, constrained, and policed. Truly, we'll find that "some friction is a natural feature of public spaces, even a good sign" (Laitio, 2022). Creating spaces that allow genuine openness means "accepting friction [as a] true test of our commitment to equity." It can make these public spaces feel more like the realities we find ourselves in when we turn to nature and bring ourselves to natural places. There's a sense of something more real behind that facade of politeness intertwined with paranoia when we find ourselves in these dead public spaces.

We do come from nature after all. We can all understand that the core human need is access to nature, to surround ourselves with plants, trees, and sunlight. However in our modern cities, we often uproot nature only to reinsert it in the form of highly organized, designated, and isolated zones scattered throughout a city or town, which we call green spaces. "Green space" is used in urban planning to denote various areas such as city parks, community or botanical gardens, and even cemeteries. In many cities, they are used sparingly and have a designated utility, whether for creating places for humans to socialize and spend time, as in parks, or simply for aesthetic reasons. Some urban planners simply believe that trees enhance aesthetics, advocating for their strategic placement around buildings and roadways, and that maybe their shade can do something nice. Green spaces are essential, and the dominant term used when talking about the need to increase access to the natural environment within the physical infrastructure of an urban city. I'm not fond of the term because I believe it isolates and artificializes nature by segregating it from its broader context. This tendency to compartmentalize is something we humans excel at in our modernity, through highly bureaucratic processes of planning and zoning. However, their significance to the human psyche cannot be understated. There's no easy way around this; we require access to natural environments, seamlessly integrated into our surroundings, rather than confined to isolated pocket parks scattered throughout the urban landscape. Access to natural spaces (yes, green spaces) is "consistently connected to improved psychological well-being, decreasing despondency, and improving intellectual working" (Siroliya, 2021). Alongside the mental health benefits, natural spaces can also help improve our "quality of social ties among neighbors by empowering utilization of basic spaces, adding to the making of sound and healthy neighborhoods." As a function of public space, natural space is the basis for how we can come together.

Just like how we thrive on our connections with nature, we also thrive on our connections to each other. Millions of people nowadays struggle with anxiety, depression, and social isolation in an increasingly online and separated world. We often find ourselves at home, alone or in the company of just one or two others, sometimes almost entirely relying on online platforms to make up for the gap in our needs for physical connection. And in our world of effects of increasing disconnection, this "social isolation is associated with decreased life satisfaction, higher levels of depression, and lower levels of psychological well-being" (Clair, 2021) and at the same time there is now "considerable evidence that social isolation can have a detrimental impact on physical health" as well. We need to be around each other, and we are craving real interactions—to converse, debate, share, engage, and love. Each day, we need to engage in these interactions within the fabric of our communities to maintain our health and happiness. People who have access to community resources and maintain them, "have satisfying relationships with family friends, and their community, are happier, have fewer health problems, and live longer" (Brody, 2017). When we spend time with one another, especially in contexts not solely focused on transactional behavior and when we do so in regular intervals throughout our lives, that "social connectedness generates a positive feedback loop of social, emotional, and physical well-being" (Brody, 2017). Public spaces are also essential for us psychologically. They can be critical to people's core identities and definitions of self. Growing up and having access to public spaces can be "psychologically significant because they are geographical spots involving complex patterns of material aspects, meanings, values, social activities, and even profound existential experiences" (Di Masso, 2012). The environments where we grow up and the spaces we spend that time in can significantly contribute to our identities as we form them throughout our lives. Public spaces can help us on an individual and a collective level to know 'who we are', by locating ourselves and others within the physical space (Di Masso, 2012). It can be psychologically significant if, growing up, the environments we have access to are dangerous, oppressive, minimized, and stressful, or if they embody a sense of safety, greenery and nature, allowance, and most importantly, conviviality. These qualities can impact how we value our place in society and each other.

By the way, what exactly is conviviality? You may have seen that word thrown in a few times so far. In one sense, conviviality means a general liveliness in social situations, but the truth is that it goes much deeper than that. The concept of conviviality, its essence, resonates more with the core philosophy behind how and why we come together as people and communities. Conviviality is our "capacity to live together", and it doesn't just refer to when we have social times that are "easy or purely positive, but rather [it means] being 'at ease' with difference. It is having the rights, skills, and resilience to act in unpredictable situations" (Laitio, 2022). To have conviviality in our lives means coming together, not as the exception in a rare outing to the public, but rather it means the essence of socialization as a regular and constant function of human life, reorienting from a life of atomization and isolation. Having that regular socialization does not just mean constant contact with friendliness, having parties and bar-hopping every night, it means learning how to share different parts of yourself with others and seeing a level of intimacy in the members of your community. It means expanding who gets to be in your community, who gets to share different parts of your life with you. To be convivial is to be brave when interacting with others. It means sharing our struggles and joys without running away back into isolation. It means that regular human interaction is happening on a societal scale, in times of love and pain, and everything in between. It means playing with others, dancing, expressing joy, cooking, drinking, and sharing. Finally, it means coming together when the hard times happen too, letting each other cry and mourn when those we love die, or when we conflict with one another because, despite everything, we remain together. Public spaces are public because that is where we find each other on common ground.

How can we get to that point? How do we facilitate the making of convivial spaces? How do we get those places in Silver City, where we can come together and express that connectedness? We now know the features these public spaces need and why we have them. Public spaces we create need to be fully public and not just a close approximation of those privately owned spaces. We need to be conscious about our design elements and make inviting features and spaces that create a sense of ease and welcome. These spaces should have access to nature embedded throughout the areas. Natural spaces can be a place to share our love for plants. These spaces should invite a general liveliness and have the ability to adapt to an extensive range of public-facing behaviors, from open-air painting classes to full-scale farmers' markets. Creating a plan will require the involvement of multiple parties if we want to change how we devel-lop our society's urban cores drastically. The development will likely require a lot of back and forth, and any plan will need to incorporate the perspectives and voices of the people who live there. One option is to take inspiration and create models from existing large-scale projects. One such project might be Atlanta's Beltline project. Atlanta's large-scale revitalization project aims at redeveloping old railways into green space, walking/biking trails, public art, and even a streetcar system, within a large circle around the city in a massive loop (Fausset, 2016) thus significantly improving upon the city's access to public space. There's an issue, though, we don't have train stations or old railways to dismantle in Silver City. What we do possess are roads ripe for reclamation from our past/current vehicular-centric approaches. Picture this more radical idea: ripping up sections of road asphalt and replacing it with bricks or blocks intertwined with plants and trees. We can turn roads into strategically placed plazas, centers, connecting walking and biking spaces. Planting desert-friendly trees and foliage down the center of that former road, and encircling the entirety of the new space with inviting walking paths, comfortable benches, and multi-use spaces for that impromptu dance party, poetry reading, or hip-hop battle. Controversially, I am proposing that this be done in the core of Silver City's downtown, on Bullard Street. This would create multifold effects that I believe will ultimately contribute to the health and well-being of our community. The public space would give rise to emergent behaviors in downtown, safe from the stress and dangers of the nearby vehicles. It would "activate" downtown in a way that hasn't been seen since Bullard Street was a dirt road. Shade structures, greenery, and benches would invite people to participate in public activities. Markets, block parties, and celebrations could be hosted safely in the street without using police to create temporary road blockades. The newly created plaza could be used as a landing to start to access more spaces outside of downtown. The walking paths of Bullard Street can lead into the adjacent trails of the

Big Ditch Park and San Vicente Creek, thus activating those spaces too. Downtown shops can see increased use and a resurgence in potential restaurants and coffee shops. We used to have a street downtown that was very much focused on highlighting this social behavior. It was called Main Street, and we lost it. We didn't lose it to car-centric ideologies or privatization; we lost it due to poor town planning and lots of rain. Floods took out our core socialization places more than one hundred years ago. So, we now have to find and rebuild those cores somewhere else.

There are a lot of legitimate concerns and logical areas for pushback when considering taking on the task of redesigning the social spaces of a town. Firstly, there is a very real cost to all this. To function, public spaces, on some level, need to be maintained. A city's municipal structure is usually involved in doing this, and it needs to be figured out what upkeep looks like and if it is worth it to the town. The irrigation of plants, the cleaning of courtyards, and the maintenance of benches and tables add up. There is a risk that time, energy, and money will be put into the creation of a public space, and it will never receive the use you thought it would. Another issue is that of cars. Vehicles would not be allowed, as cars present a real and stressful danger to walking persons, and that can be an issue for some. If those public spaces are created by dismantling roads and taking up street space, parking is still an issue. All the new public spaces in the world still won't fix the problem of transportation at the core. New public spaces don't mean that car infrastructure for transport magically vanishes. The issues of cars will need to be resolved alongside the planning and activation of public spaces. We need new modes of transport that are economical, inclusive, and widely available for people to come and go from these public spaces, but that can be the subject of an entirely different research essay. Another issue is that of gentrification. Many criticize Atlanta's Beltline project for contributing to aspects of gentrification at the same time that it is creating

The advent of the Beltline has "driven up housing costs on nearby land and pushed low-income households out to suburbs with fewer services than downtown neighborhoods" (Immergluck, 2024) Economic exploration and policies need to be put in place so that while we improve our infrastructure and urban environments, we don't end up kicking out those who belong here by making the price to live inaccessible. Finally, is the issue of having homeless people exist in these public spaces too? Here's the thing: having public spaces means you cannot control who uses them. They are for everybody, and that means everybody. When we go out, we do run the risk of interacting with potentially dangerous people as well as homeless people. But those are not the same group of people. You find homeless people in public spaces often, obviously to the point where designers find it necessary, in their worldview, to install anti-homeless spikes. But this is because the public spaces are the only places that many homeless people even have access to. Being homeless means just that, you don't have a home to return to when you are done using the public space. Engaging in public spaces means engaging with sketchy people that can be scary, but they are going to be here no matter what, and our public spaces shouldn't suffer because somebody is finding a temporary bed in a bench. It is the essence of conviviality that we act in joy and connection, even when certain people scare us from time to time. We should make our public spaces feel comfortable and safe for all, including those who are homeless; they need that safety and comfort too, probably more than the rest of us. We need to do better as a society to deal with the issue of homelessness as a separate but connected issue to that of public spaces, another topic worthy of a lengthy research paper for sure.

Despite all the challenges of building new public spaces, and there are many, they are essential to the continued well-being and safety of our human societies. The world is already a tough place, and many stressful events happen regularly, whether it's political upheaval, climate crisis, forgein government, or civil war; these are all causing us to feel anxious, unsafe, and uncertain. But I am dreaming of places to engage with the world and spend time with the people I love and care about. A world where I am surrounded by environments that are real and grounded, and I feel safe to exist. I dream of places where I can go outside to paint and draw because the plants and trees next to the buildings are just so interesting. I can hear guitars and fiddles playing beside the plant beds in the streets. I meet new community members and talk about books, political ideas, or philosophy. I introduce myself to people like me and people unlike me. Older generations can walk up and down the block, and children can run around, weaving between benches, planters, and sculptures. I dream of spaces where I can sit and play chess with my friends and drink coffee under the sun, surrounded by the sounds of branches moving in the wind, birdsong. There is the sound of chats between old friends talking about schools and sunsets, bikes rolling past down the path. Places where our meetings and get-togethers can be under the stars or in the shade of a hot summer, but we remain safe and connected within the hearts of our communities — because we understand that these spaces are ours.

)

References:

Allen, R. M. (2021, November 5). The road to ruin — how the car drove US cities to the brink. Financial Times. https://www.ft.com/content/27169841-7ee3-481e-919d-41b247e401f6

Brody, J. E. (2017, June 12). Having friends is good for you. The New York Times. https://www.nytimes.com/2017/06/12/well/live/having-friends-is-good-for-you.html

Di Masso, A. (2012, February 23). Grounding citizenship: Toward a political psychology of public space. Political Psychology, 33(1), 123–143. https://doi.org/10.1111/j.1467-9221.2011.00866.x

Clair, R., Gordon, M., Kroon, M., et al. (2021). The effects of social isolation on well-being and life sat isfaction during pandemic. Humanities & Social Sciences Communications. https://doi.org/10.1057/s41599-021-00710-3

Fausset, R. (2016, September 11). Atlanta BeltLine: A Billion-Dollar Project, a Harsh Reality. The New York Times. https://www.nytimes.com/2016/09/12/us/atlanta-beltline.html

Garrett, B. L. (2015, August 4). The privatization of cities' public spaces is escalating. It is time to take a stand. The Guardian. ttps://www.theguardian.com/cities/2015/aug/04/pops-privately-owned-public-space-cities -direct-action

Hu, W. (2019, November 8). Hostile Architecture in New York City: What It Is and Why It's Unfair. The New York Times. https://www.nytimes.com/2019/11/08/nyregion/hostile- architecture-nyc.html

Immergluck, D. (2024, February 6). Atlanta's beltline shows how urban parks can drive "green gentrification" if cities don't think about affordable housing at the start. The Conversation. https://theconversation.com/atlantas-beltline-shows-how-urban-parks-can-drive-green-gentrification-if-cities-dont-think-about-affordable-housing-at-the-start-193204

Laitio, T. (2022, November 29). Learning Grounds for Conviviality. Johns Hopkins University Center for Government Excellence. https://publicinnovation.jhu.edu/learning-grounds-for-conviviality/

Melosi, M. V. (n.d.). The Automobile Shapes The City. http://www.autolife.umd.umich.edu/Environment/E_Casestudy/E_casestudy.htm

Siroliya, Y. (2021, November 22). The psychological impact of public spaces on city dwellers. RTF | Rethinking The Future. https://www.re-thinkingthefuture.com/rtf-fresh-perspectives/a1353-the-psychological-im pact-of-public-spaces-on-city-dwellers/

Wiseman, E. (2024, January 21). Hostile architecture is making our cities even less welcoming. The Guardian. https://www.theguardian.com/lifeandstyle/2024/jan/21/hostile-architecture-is-making-our -cities-even-less-welcoming

Innocence

Autumn Ellis-Ward

I see it in your eyes

The love I have for you

I will keep you safe

To start a life and learn to grow

The love I have for you

One day you will be gone

To start a life and learn to grow

The innocence I see

One day you will be gone

The day you were born

The innocence I see

A warm bundle that I hold

The day you were born

I will keep you safe

A warm bundle that I hold

I see it in your eyes

Her Essence

Autumn Ellis-Ward

The woman was wise.

She had silver hair that once was fire red—

Speak the truth, but only of the good in others,

where I am you have a home.

She had silver hair that once was fire red—

Hello darling,

where I am you have a home.

I hear the wind through the phone, are you outside?

Hello darling,

the roses are growing.

I hear the wind through the phone, are you outside?

How are you doing?

The roses are growing./

Speak the truth, but only of the good in others—

How are you doing?

The woman was wise.

Sun

Danisha Garcia

Warm is the mark left by the mother sandal
As she told me to calm down, I was too wild.

My father kept silent, staying in the corner,
later bringing popsicles to my room, one for us both

Tan, not burnt, my cheeks were still red,
from the sun's relentless rays.

Sweat rolled off my face, mixed with tears,
I'll never return home again.

Edges of Truth: The Boundaries of Humanity in Antigone and Frankstein

Gabe Farley

Western New Mexico University

ALAS 1810

To confront the inevitability of death is to grapple with one of life's most fundamental truths. These are themes that define both Sophocles' Antigone and Mary Shelley's Frankenstein. Antigone's defiant burial of Polyneices asserts an eternal truth: that divine law and the sacredness of death supersede human authority. Her actions reveal truth not as mutable policy but as the immutable order of nature itself. Victor Frankenstein, by stark contrast, distorts truth through scientific ambition, treating mortality not as a boundary to respect but as a frontier to conquer. Where Antigone's obedience to divine truth leads her to embrace her fate, Victor's rejection of natural truth brings only suffering. Their stories form a conversation about the nature of truth: Antigone demonstrates how truth is discovered through submission to cosmic order, while Victor shows how truth is obscured by the pride of those attempting to master nature and impose the Enlightenment sensibility of science over reality. Through these opposing relationships with mortality, Antigone and Frankenstein ultimately argue that truth resides in recognizing and yielding to the unchangeable laws that govern life and death.

Antigone's defiance of Creon's rule, by leaving Polyneices' body unburied, transcends mere rebellion; it embodies her fidelity to the sacred laws of death, which the Greeks saw as foundational to both cosmic order and human dignity. The Greek pantheon, often personifying Natural Law, reinforces the truth that these principles exist beyond mortal decrees. When Creon confronts Antigone for breaking his law, she responds, "Zeus did not announce those laws to me. And Justice living with the gods below sent no such laws for men. I did not think anything which you proclaimed strong enough to let a mortal override the gods and their unwritten and unchanging laws" (line 508). Here, Antigone exposes the fragility of human authority when measured against divine truth. Her unwavering commitment to Natural Law, even unto death, starkly contrasts with Creon's hypocritical policies, revealing how truth becomes corrupted when severed from the natural world. As Edmund Stewart, Assistant Professor in Ancient Greek History at the University of Nottingham writes, "Perhaps that an idea that is popular or new is not always right; that what we knew to be true yesterday cannot be easily unlearned today; that what is expedient is not always just; that sometimes it is better to speak the truth, even at the risk of causing offence; and, yes, that there is much worth living for – and if necessary, worth dying for as well." In this light, Antigone becomes not just a tragic figure but a philosopher of the absolute, measuring human laws against the unchanging metrics of divine truth, the ultimate truth of the reality of death.

While Antigone affirms truth through her submission to natural law, Victor Frankenstein's tragedy emerges from his radical denial of these same boundaries. Where Antigone recognizes death as a sacred threshold and an ultimate truth, Victor sees only an obstacle to be conquered through scientific ambition, to push and defy this sense of truth. "...treading in the steps already marked, I will pioneer a new way, explore unknown powers, and unfold to the world the deepest mysteries of creation" (pg. 29). Though framed as noble truth-seeking, this proclamation gradually reveals itself as an anxious attempt to control the fundamental forces of existence. As the narrative unfolds, Victor's obsession with 'unfolding creation's mysteries' devolves into a desperate struggle against the very truths Antigone reveres, exposing

Enlightenment ambition as not just hubris, but fundamentally fearful of nature's immutable laws. His creation of the Creature violates the fundamental truth Antigone defends: that life and death exist in a balance no mortal should disrupt. The Creature itself becomes the embodied consequence of this violated truth. He states, "I, the miserable and the abandoned, am an abortion, to be spurned at, and kicked, and trampled on. Even now my blood boils at the recollection of this injustice" (pg. 146). Unlike Antigone, whose actions expose Creon's hypocrisy, Victor's experiments reveal the dangerous fallacy of Enlightenment rationality, of pushing against real boundaries. "The monstrous creation becomes a cautionary tale, illustrating the horrifying effects of an ideology that prioritises unchecked rationality over humane considerations" (Poorghorban, Y., & Taghizadeh, A., 2023). Ultimately, both works arrive at the same conclusion through opposite paths: that truth exists independent of human will and attempts to redefine or dominate it lead only to ruin.

The tragic outcomes for both protagonists, Antigone's permanent defiance and Victor's psychological collapse, reveal a shared warning about the consequences of humanity's relationship with truth. Antigone's suicide, far from a surrender, becomes the ultimate affirmation of her adherence to divine law and the truth. In death, she embodies the Greek ideal that truth is realized through harmony with cosmic truth, not defiance of it, her last words: "Look on me, you lords of Thebes,... the kind of men who do this to me, for paying reverence to true piety" (line 1053). Victor, by contrast, survives his creation only to become a hollow shell, his dying words: "I myself have been blasted in these hopes, yet another may succeed" (pg. 146), exposing the delusion that truth can be rewritten through more Enlightenment-formed thinking. Antigone's truth is relational: honoring bonds between the living, the dead, and the gods, while Victor's is transactional: seeking to extract nature's secrets without reciprocity or cohesion. Together, the texts frame truth not as abstract knowledge but as a moral compass: Antigone's compass points to reverence, Victor's to ruin. A skeptic might argue that Frankenstein's warning against scientific overreach is outdated. After all, modern medicine has successfully pushed against natural limits of the era, curing diseases, extending life, and even reviving clinically dead patients through advanced resuscitation. If Victor Frankenstein's sin was defying mortality, then are today's scientists similarly guilty with the precision of modern surgery? Similarly, one could dismiss Antigone's "divine law" as mere ancient mythology: Zeus and the Olympians no more dictate cosmic truth than Frankenstein's alchemy mirrors modern biology. Why should we put Sophocles' plays on a theistic pedestal over humanity's demonstrable progress? Yet this objection misreads both texts. Frankenstein critiques not science itself, but the hubris of pursuing knowledge without ethical responsibility. This warning resonates in debates over AI, genetic engineering, and advanced technological/societal engineering existent in the modern smartphone. Meanwhile, Antigone's "divine law" is less about literal gods than the moral absolutes that sustain civilization: respect for the dead, the bonds of kinship, and humility before forces greater than ourselves. Modern science has indeed conquered many frontiers, but not the existential truth both works uphold: that some boundaries, whether ethical (cloning, as referenced in Brave New World), ecological (environmental collapse), or ontological (death itself), demand reverence, not conquest or domination. The fact that we no longer attribute these truths to Olympus doesn't negate their power; it simply means we must rediscover them through reason and access to our deeper senses of intuition rather than religious myth or revelation. We have and will continue to push boundaries in the various fields of science, but that boundary pushing doesn't deny the presence of a greater truth, of natural laws of life and death, and the modern world does have a hard time dealing with those truths.

Antigone and Frankenstein are not merely stories of ancient rebellion or Gothic horror; they are urgent blueprints for navigating our own era of exponential scientific and social upheaval. If we dismiss Antigone's "divine law" as obsolete mythology or Victor's breakdown as simple mental illness/paranoia, we risk repeating their tragedies in modern form: gene-edited babies, AI systems built without ethical constraints, and climate interventions that treat Earth as a laboratory rather than a sacred home. As Audrey Shafer, MD puts it in an article for Stanford Magazine, "[When] the frontiers are pushed further and further, the unintended consequences of how science and technology are used could affect who we are as humans, the viability of our planet and how society evolves" (2018). However, we do not need to go the opposite route in re-creating mythologies that we rigidly adhere to, perceiving natural forces as human personifications again. These texts compel us to ask what we've sacrificed in our pursuit of progress. Like Creon and Victor, we stand at a precipice where power threatens to outpace principle. The stakes are no longer theatrical but existential. Our choices will determine whether we honor the sacred (whether framed as divine, ecological, or humanistic) or fracture it and ourselves beyond repair. Let these stories be our caution and our compass: truth is not ours to invent, but to discover and defend, and maybe to keep discovering where the edges lie. Death is a fundamental aspect of truth and must be honored and respected, in whatever ways we as humans deem necessary to ritualize. As much as reality-disconnected tech bros seem to think we can live in a world without it, death remains an essential aspect of our shared human world.

Clair, R., Gordon, M., Kroon, M., et al. (2021). The effects of social isolation on well-being and life satisfaction during pandemic. Humanities & Social Sciences Communications. https://doi.org/10.1057/s41599-021-00710-3

Fausset, R. (2016, September 11). Atlanta BeltLine: A Billion-Dollar Project, a Harsh Reality. The New York Times. https://www.nytimes.com/2016/09/12/us/atlanta-beltline.html

Garrett, B. L. (2015, August 4). The privatization of cities' public spaces is escalating. It is time to take a stand. The Guardian. ttps://www.theguardian.com/cities/2015/aug/04/pops-privately-owned-public-space-cities -direct-action

Hu, W. (2019, November 8). Hostile Architecture in New York City: What It Is and Why It's Unfair. The New York Times. https://www.nytimes.com/2019/11/08/nyregion/hostile-architecture-nyc.html

Immergluck, D. (2024, February 6). Atlanta's beltline shows how urban parks can drive "green gentrification" if cities don't think about affordable housing at the start. The Conversation. https://theconversation.com/atlantas-beltline-shows-how-urban-parks-can-drive-green-gentrification-if-cities-dont-think-about-affordable-housing-at-the-start-193204

Laitio, T. (2022, November 29). Learning Grounds for Conviviality. Johns Hopkins University Center for Government Excellence. https://publicinnovation.jhu.edu/learning-grounds-for-conviviality/

I Want To Hold Her Hand

Natalie Ann Preito

There is a little girl.

She is five years old.

I owe her so much.

I often forget She is around,

Think of Her as I do,

I neglect Her all the same.

I am so hard on Her.

She shares My exact smile

And the knowing look in Her eye

Is one I catch in the rearview mirror

As we exchange the car seat for the driver's side.

We look different and the same.

Who are you now?

It is sometimes hard to hold Her gaze for too long.

Her little back carries the world and holds Me with it –
Atlas Telamon of Her own free will with no one to take it
away.
Her hands dig into the Earth,
Muddied and caked,
Grasping for something it seems everyone has forgotten.
She holds up the clay She has found to show Me.
We can both be molded, Her Cheshire Cat grin seems to say,
But We can always come back.
We are both the same.

There is a little girl.
She was born with an instinct,
With everything I ever needed to know loaded into Her
mind,
Her heart, Her soul.

I often hear Her calling or tugging at My shirt.
Just look, just wait, is all She seems to say.

I fear I run too far and too fast for Her to keep up.
We are different, but I am wrong.

I, the grown woman who claims to know so much and so
better,
Yet realized only just today how
I love holding hands and waking up early –
Lying in bed with sunshine pouring in
And rolling down hills, grass stuck in my hair and nose.

Laughing for the joy of it and loving just because.
Being held and not hurt.
We can always come back; we can always return.

There is a little girl.
She knows what We need.

But She is only five.
And She is reaching out to me.
I think, finally,
I want to hold her hand.

THE MAVERICK EDITORS' FEATURE II

The Ingenious Diets of the Indigenous: Looking Back as a Way Forward for the Health of America

Arielle Certosimo

English 1120

Western New Mexico University

The Paleolithic diet, also known as the Paleo or caveman diet, is focused on the consumption of foods that human beings ate during the Paleolithic era as hunter gatherers. The Paleolithic era lasted from 2.8 million years ago until 12,000 BC (de la O et al., 2021). The diet of the hunter gatherers during this period and therefore the foods that make up the Paleo diet include whole, unprocessed foods such as meat, fish, eggs, vegetables, fruits, nuts, seeds, and natural sweeteners such as honey and maple syrup; and exclude processed foods, grains, legumes, dairy and refined sugars. The introduction of agriculture and subsequently the more frequent consumption of non-Paleo-deemed foods allegedly seem to coincide with when the health of human beings began to decline. The Paleo diet continues to be of interest to people and researchers, especially considering the prolific chronic disease epidemic of today and the general unhealthiness of the population. A Paleo diet is commonly considered healthy and is rising in popularity, although it might seem unsustainable to some.

Leaving out certain food groups can certainly seem daunting as grains and dairy especially are ingrained in cultures across the globe. Often grains are a staple in any given diet and are eaten in abundance around the world. There are massive and powerful farming operations behind the production, sale, and processing of grains. For a long time, grains were even touted as the largest and most important part of the diet according to government food pyramids and recommendations. The Paleo diet could be considered controversial due to its under-reliance on big corporations processed and fortified agricultural products. The strong presence of animal meats and fats in contrast to the explosion of plant-based, vegan, and vegetarian movements could be a point of contention; or there could simply be confusion due to years of misguided public policies emphasizing the nutritional need for an abundance of grains in a healthy diet.

The benefits of knowing more about the Paleo diet and its effects on the human body include reduction or possibly reversal of chronic diseases, improving personal health outcomes and those of future generations, strengthening personal health autonomy and responsibility by putting disease management in the hands of the individual, learning about what foods are most nutrient dense, and relieving the burden of medical doctors and hospitals that spend so much time and money treating, or trying to treat chronic diseases that may be more efficiently managed with diet and lifestyle. Health can truly be wealth when health care costs are exponentially cut. The risks of ignoring the importance of the Paleo diet and instead continuing to provide short term solutions to chronic disease in the form of pharmaceutical drugs would be detrimental. This would further create discrepancies in public health policy, recommendations and science when it comes to food. Chronic disease could affect even more people than it does today, quality of life could decrease, and the power of and reliance on pharmaceutical companies to "solve" diseases would increase.

The modern hype for the Paleo diet is based on the idea of evolutionary health promotion, or the concept that human beings' diets have evolved faster than our genetics can catch up (de la O et al., 2021).

Given the rising rates of disease and death in current times since the industrial agricultural revolution, this concept may give way to an explanation for the general health decline of human beings. Returning to the eating habits of our Paleolithic ancestors could very well solve the chronic disease epidemic quite simply. Americans deserve to live long healthy lives, and the Paleo diet is ideal to become the basic framework for food recommendations, especially for chronic disease management. The ingenious indigenous ways of Paleolithic ancestors could help society move forward by looking backwards.

Many novel diseases that plague society today such as heart disease, diabetes, and cancer are considered civilization-related diseases (Pontzer & Wood, 2021). This means that chronic conditions are caused by some modern lifestyle factor since these diseases simply did not exist in the Paleolithic era and do not exist presently in hunter gatherer cultures of today. One emerging scientific approach that examines this disparity between the health of populations looks at modern day hunter gatherers, sustenance farmers and horticulturists since they are extraordinarily resistant to civilization-related diseases (Pontzer & Wood, 2021). Furthermore, these populations maintain a diet and activity level that is consistent with Paleolithic ancestors; a lifestyle that is highly active with a minimally processed whole foods diet that seems to protect these populations against civilization related diseases (Pontzer & Wood, 2021). Looking at the lifestyles of modern-day hunter gatherers helps to give insight into the lifestyles of those who characterized our evolutionary past.

More than 600,000 years ago, Paleolithic humans were consistently hunting large mammals and cooking food using fire, making it much more easily digestible (Pontzer & Wood, 2021). Usually, men in the community were the ones hunting and the women in the community were the ones gathering plant foods. Foods were shared within the community which significantly decreased the risk of food shortages weren't successful in making a kill. The symbiosis of the roles and food sharing in the community provided the nutrient density of meats while mitigating its ecological risks by having back up foods that were gathered, resulting in making hunter gatherers extremely successful throughout the Paleolithic, and eventually expanding the human species to every corner of the planet (Pontzer & Wood, 2021). Herman Pontzer and Brian Wood, anthropologists from Duke University and the University of California published their insights from information both new and compiled over a 25-year period observing these modern hunter gatherer societies and comparing them to recent archeological data from the Paleolithic era. They focused on the Hazda, a hunter gatherer community located in Northern Tanzania. What they found is that the diets of the Hazda are incredibly varied, with plants, animals, honey, nuts, seeds and other foods (even wild rice) contributing to their diets and leading to a variation in macronutrient intake. While they found that tubers and root vegetables are at least 1,000 times more plentiful than mammalian prey, the fact that meat still contributed substantially to their diet indicates an inclination towards meat over calories derived from plants while still making calculated and lifesaving gathering choices, like collecting tubers (2021). Plant Underground Storage Organs, or foods like tubers, bulbs, and roots are critical to hunter gatherers in tropical and temperate regions who use these foods for survival or as a fall-back food when there are food shortages of other more nutritionally dense foods or when their preferred foods are unavailable (2021). Hunter gatherers also eagerly consume nuts and seeds in abundance which provide a healthy balance of fat, protein and carbohydrates. Not only are the types of foods extremely varied, but the amounts of different food groups are consumed in differing quantities seasonally and, when considering other similar communities across the planet, location is a factor in the variety and abundance of certain foods during certain times.

Those who live in colder climates like the Arctic consume more meat and fish while those who live in tropical climates consume more plants overall (2021). The health outcomes of modern-day hunter gatherers are influenced by the food variety over time and location, as well as the types of foods these communities favor.

Sociocultural factors also influence food choice. Eva C. Monterrosa, PhD from The Global Alliance for Improved Nutrition in Geneva, Switzerland and her co-authors created a comprehensive look into what drives food preferences in response to a call for dietary transformations from the global policy discourse on sustainability and health (2020). Monterrosa et al. refer to sociocultural food practices as "… material and ideational (cognitive) elements that give rise to specific dietary patterns within a geographic region or social group" (2020). The values that contribute to how people view and choose food are factors like location, naturalness, taste, appearance, cost, comfort, convenience, tradition/food symbolism, social relationships, nutrition, safety, variety, environmental impact, origin, and ethics (2020). Food choices are also affected by biology or how genetics influence the way a person experiences taste (2020). Some foods are pleasurable on the palate such as fat, and especially when paired with sugar (2020). Food companies have been accused of taking advantage of our biological predispositions by creating foods high in fat, sugar and salt that appeal to the pleasure receptors in the brain (2020).

When Pozner and Wood looked at studies of the Hazdas' blood test results from around 50 years ago, they revealed low cholesterol levels and almost no hypertension was detected, even among the elderly. Their recent findings are completely aligned with the studies from half a century ago, meaning the health of the Hazda population has not worsened over time like Americans' health has. However, these health outcomes could potentially be due to another factor such as lower stress levels or other lifestyle factors that could have been overlooked. Pozner and Wood maintain that "The mix of foods in the Hadza diet, together with their high volume of daily physical activity, appears to provide a nutritional framework that supports excellent cardiometabolic health" (Pontzer & Wood, 2021). Interestingly, the evidence suggests that it is not necessarily a sedentary lifestyle that is the main contributor to obesity among industrialized populations, but recent changes in food intake seem to be the most significant driver of obesity. Although the Hazda and other small-scale communities maintain high levels of physical activity, their total daily energy expenditures still match the more sedentary populations (Pontzer & Wood, 2021). Because hunter gatherer populations consume a significantly higher proportion of wild foods which are far more nutritionally dense than domesticated foods, it could be that this alone influences hunger and satiety, rather than the types of foods themselves that protect the hunter-gatherer population against obesity and other diseases so effectively. Dietary diversity appears to play a role in universal avoidance of non-communicable diseases within modern hunter gatherer communities. In addition, subsistence farmers and pastoralist communities are similarly healthy (Pontzer & Wood, 2021).

Another point of interest is the health of the gut microbiome in hunter gatherer societies compared to that of those living in an industrialized society. Researchers are beginning to connect poor gut health to a whole host of diseases, from mental health disorders to cancer and every inflammatory condition in between. A recent study was done that extracted DNA from 14 archeological stool samples including the oldest known human fecal matter extracted from El Salt, Spain; and then compared the beneficial gut bacteria species with those of the gut microbiomes from modern humans with much different dietary patterns. These groups included the Hazdas and Matses hunter gatherers, Tunapuco rural agriculturists and Western urbans from Italy and the US. The study found that the ancestral El Salt samples resemble the Matses and Tunapuco more closely; and that there are certain bacteria present in samples of ancient people's gut microbiomes that are missing from Western people's gut microbiomes (Rampelli et al., 2021). The researchers also found that declining amounts of these certain bacteria coincide with the rise of auto-immune and inflammatory issues among Westerners (2021). Furthermore, they noted that cholesterol-reducing bacteria detected in the ancient samples indicate that higher cholesterol intake has been an important part of the human diet and a crucial function of the gut microbiome since at least the Middle Pleistocene (2021). The researchers concluded that in the US today, there is a loss of bacterial diversity in the gut microbiome with a subsequent rise in autoimmune and inflammatory disorders directly related to the health of the gut microbiome (2021).

Considering how the Paleo diet influences the excellent health of modern and ancient hunter gatherers, it is important to also look at research on how the Paleo diet affects the modern person living in an industrialized society. Sticking to a Paleo diet greatly reduces the risk of breast cancer, as one 2023 study shows (Sohouli et al., 2023); and a separate 2023 study's findings suggest that adhering to the Paleo diet and Paleo lifestyle could be a new option to reduce colorectal cancer (Xiao et al., 2023). The Paleo diet has a positive effect on diabetes and insulin resistance. A 2021 study found that a Paleo diet is associated with "a decrease in fat mass, body weight, waist circumference, systolic blood pressure, and triglyceride levels among patients with type 2 diabetes" (Mårtensson et al., 2021). A study, although done on domestic pigs and not humans, suggests that a Paleo diet granted a "higher insulin sensitivity, lower C-reactive protein and lower blood pressure when compared to a cereal based diet" (Jönsson et al., 2006). Another recent study focused on Paleolithic Diet Fractions (PDFs) which is the portion of a person's diet that comes from foods that are considered Paleo (Rydhög et al., 2023). Higher PDFs were associated with "healthier levels of cardiometabolic risk factors such as glycemic control, waist circumference, body weight and blood lipids" (Rydhög et al., 2023). The researchers found that a high PDF lowered the risk of death from all causes, including but not limited to death related to tumors, the cardiovascular system, the respiratory system, neurological related deaths, and digestive disease (2023).

Modern, westernized food is nutritionally affected by farming. The nutritional dissimilarities between wild and farmed foods must be taken into account when considering modern hunter gatherer societies and how that data may inform public health policy choices. Farming practices alter the nutritional make up of plants and animals since they have been artificially selected to "increase energy content, decrease fiber content, or both" according to Pontzer & Wood (2021). A lot of the farmed foods Americans eat only offer 1/10th the amount of fiber of the same plant the Hadzas eat but with the same or in even some cases double the carbohydrate content (Pontzer & Wood, 2021). This could mean that for Americans, since farmed foods are an overwhelming majority of what is consumed, an increase of carbohydrates is dominating the standard American diet. Furthermore, farming focuses on producing more of a plant or say, more grains per plant rather than worrying about the nutritional density and diversity of the plant. Wild foods are consistently much more nutritionally dense than domesticated ones (Pontzer & Wood, 2021). Similar nutritional deficiencies are present in domesticated animals versus their more nutritionally dense and varied wild counterparts. Studies found that wild game contained 50% less fat stores on average than farm animals. In addition, when looking at the fat content found in lean muscle in wild game mammals, it was also 50% less than that of farm raised animals (Pontzer & Wood, 2021). When the whole animal is consumed, this means that a farm animal has twice as much fat as a wild animal does and a substantially greater portion of carbohydrates. (Pontzer & Wood, 2021). This leads to the question of whether or not the farm animals included in this study were primarily grain fed. It is interesting to note that a study done on laboratory raised pigs showed that fatty acid profiles were like those of wild warthog and differed from farmed pigs. This implies that farming practices do indeed play a significant role in the nutritional outcomes of meat (Pontzer & Wood, 2021). Pozner and Wood warned, "…Paleo diets popular in industrialized populations today are unlikely to converge nutritionally on the diets of ancestral hunter-gatherers, because the foods available in grocery stores and farmers markets are qualitatively different from wild foods" (2021).

The strongest factors contributing to the declining health of the nation seem to be modern farming practices that potentially prioritize the more cost-effective option of grain feeding the animals vs the more nutritionally dense/balanced outcomes of grass fed and/or pasture raised meat. The standard American diet (SAD) which is already unproportionately higher in carbohydrates is exacerbated by the higher carbohydrate content found in farmed foods and animals, foods that are expected to contribute to optimal health. The lack of wild foods present in the SAD could leave the population somewhat nutritionally depleted, and the lack of variety of foods could be contributing to loss of westerners' gut biodiversity. Of these obstacles, farming practices seem to be most resistant to change, simply because the big business of agriculture works very much like the big business of anything else – to cut corners financially wherever possible in order to increase profits. The goal of these massive farming operations isn't to increase the health or wellness of the population, unfortunately, and their decisions lay solely with financial outcomes and quantity of products sold. Another obstacle that is embedded in society is now the reliance on, and preference for foods that differ greatly from what modern and/or ancient hunter gatherer societies preferred to eat. Many Americans prefer processed, grain-based foods out of convenience, cost, familiarity, comfort, or perhaps the biochemically addictive nature of the foods. It could certainly be a challenge to shift the food preferences and choices of the average American at this stage in the game. There are many misconceptions about the Paleo diet due to outdated assumptions and biases. For example, a lot of people think that the Paleo diet excludes all carbohydrates, including fruits and vegetables, due to there not being archaeological evidence for plants in the recent past. Bones, tools and other evidence of hunting preserve better than plant matter. However, it is now widely accepted and scientifically proven that plants are and were in fact an important part of the diets, lifestyles, and cultural practices of hunter gatherers; as well as plants being medicinally significant to these societies (Hardy, et al., 2022). There are also some inherent biases present in the idea that the Paleo diet is meat focused given that the data from the past was collected and recorded by males; and when considering the roles of hunter gatherers, where the men hunt, and the women gather there could have been attention placed on hunting rather than gathering. Research has been skewed because a lot of data and archeological evidence came from Northern locations that were colder and relied more on fish and animal meats and fats while warmer, more tropical regions that relied more on plants were sooner to be taken over by farming so less evidence survived. The somewhat newly emerging picture of plants being a part of the diet explains where other calories and survival may have come from and paints a more balanced picture of the diets of ancient people. Interestingly, the Paleo diet usually excludes certain tubers and roots such as white potatoes, but evidence shows otherwise that these food groups are indeed important and necessary for survival for hunter gatherers (Pontzer & Wood, 2021). It is interesting to note the consumption of wild grains within the Hazda communities, as grains are not included in what is today understood as a Paleo diet. However, there is an important distinction here and that is the quantity and quality of grains consumed.

However, there is an important distinction here and that is the quantity and quality of grains consumed. As mentioned by Pozner & Wood, the Hazdas prefer meat, and seem to use starches and grains as back up or survival foods. This is in sharp contrast to the SAD, which is composed mainly of carbohydrate-heavy processed foods, and Americans heavily favor grains. Of course, the nutritional profiles of wild grains vary greatly from the ones found at supermarkets in America.

Although the conclusions made by Pontzer & Wood seem to paint a dismal "don't even try" picture when it comes to matching the diet of hunter gatherer societies, there may be more to consider. For one, America mustn't take an all or nothing approach when it comes to health, not in this dire of a chronic disease epidemic. Even though America will very likely never match the intake and variety of wild foods that hunter gatherers do, studies still do show that eating a Paleo diet, farmed foods and all, cuts down civilization-related diseases quite effectively. In comparing Pontzer & Wood's proverbial shrugging of the shoulders to Karen Hardy's conclusion, (Professor of Prehistoric Archaeology at the University of Glasgow) Hardy's recommendations for reconstructing the Paleo diet include carbohydrates and framing nutritional requirements first on the needs of reproducing females and highly active individuals and then taking into account archaeological and biomolecular evidence (Hardy et al., 2022). If the Paleo diet guidelines that researchers have used in studies that examine the relationship between civilization related diseases and the Paleo diet as constructed in those studies show such remarkable results, it would be wise to use those guidelines as a general framework with implied leniency on adding well selected, preferably wild grains on occasion. There should be different guidelines for disease management that would include a stricter ban on grains and starches, at least until the patient is in remission. Rather than searching for a cure for cancer, how about utilizing already established ways of preventing cancer? Doesn't it make more sense to prevent the disease rather than treat it once it has already wreaked havoc in the body? Of course it does, but unfortunately pharmaceutical companies have a choke hold on advancements in medical science and an emphasis is always placed on treatment rather than prevention.

In conclusion, it is essential that knowledge of the health benefits of the Paleo diet become widely known. This should be a foundational and historical element to doctor's education in medical school, and emphasis should be placed on nutrition taking center stage in the role of disease management. This would create a chain reaction of doctors advising appropriate nutrition guidelines for schools, hospitals, cancer centers, and for the nation in general. But in order for this to happen, there would need to be an established and agreed-upon framework for what the Paleo diet consists of. Policy planning should also include thorough sociocultural analysis to figure out how accepted this change would be across different cultures and what influence and language would look like to make a shift like this successful. Doing this analysis based on groups or locations instead of the country as a whole could be beneficial to properly include elements of locality and culture (Monterrosa et al., 2020). Hopefully with some of the research, information, and ideas compiled in this paper, other researchers have begun to put the pieces together and that can become a reality in the near future. Americans may also consider taking charge of their health by making a point to connect with their ancestral roots. Discovering local, wild foods may be spiritually and physically significant given the higher nutritional profile of wild foods and the act of being in nature and gathering foods that grow locally. For example, here in Southwestern New Mexico, mesquite is a plant that is seasonally harvested and then milled into a flour. There are community events surrounding and celebrating the harvesting and milling of mesquite, followed by a wild foods breakfast where mesquite flour pancakes are the star. Cultivating more of these types of events around the country would be beneficial to connect people to their health and locale. This idea would be difficult to implement in larger cities, but interested parties may consider forming groups that are interested in wild foods and make it a point to visit somewhere that could provide that opportunity. Dandelions even grow out of sidewalk cracks in the cities, though it is not advised to eat a city sidewalk dandelion. Policy planning and design relies on thoroughly analyzing food values. The importance of these values lies in their capacity to create strong emotional ties to food and encapsulate culturally relevant ideas and beliefs that can be used to meet goals toward healthier, more sustainable food choices that could change food norms and promote healthier modes of existence (Monterrosa et al., 2020). Monterrosa et al. emphasizes the importance of analyzing food values. "Values may help create stories, myths, and narratives because values capture deep, universal truths. Emotions and forging emotional connections are indispensable for creating promotional campaigns that motivate consumers toward health and sustainability" (2020). Movements toward healthier food choices are already underway, creating new cultural identities and shared emotional experiences (2020). Some examples of these movements are the organic food movement and the slow food movement in which shoppers use different sets of values to inform their food purchases (2020). However, these movements have been criticized as only feasible for the wealthy or privileged (2020). Monterrosa et al. observed that "The return to traditional cuisines values how food is produced, creating emotional linkages with the cuisine of the past" (2020). Returning to traditional cuisines of the past as well as a push toward deemphasizing or eliminating processed foods is already a part of new food guidelines in Latin America, Brazil, and Uruguay (2020).

Integrating the Paleo diet into public health and nutrition of modern industrialized America will require the same adaptability that ancient hunter gatherers displayed which allowed them to expand across the globe. Adaptability means diversity and realizing that humans can be healthy on a broad range of different foods, so what works for one person, or a group of people may not work for the next. One recurring theme in many of the research journals cited in this paper is the variability of what foods are consumed based on location and what is seasonally available. It might be beneficial to create food guidelines that are tailored to specific locations, riding on the coattails of "locavores" or the local food movement. Blanket recommendations may be easiest to formulate but may not be as effective at promoting optimal health. As Pontzer and Wood suggest, Americans must move beyond the recommendations of types of foods and focus more on the nutritional profiles of foods if we are to attempt to emulate the diets and stellar health of hunter gatherers (2021). Wild foods are higher in protein, fiber, and micronutrients than farmed foods are and it would be wise to emphasize those elements of wild foods. This in turn would increase satiety, decrease weight gain, and ward off civilization related diseases, promoting optimal health for Americans. It would be beneficial to include Paleolithic Diet Fractions (PDFs) or play with those percentages in food diet recommendations to make it more appealing and sustainable. Society makes it seem like the next invention or advancement in technology will give us the answer or the cure, when the answer has always been there but has been overlooked. Lastly, for those reading this that may feel intimidated about starting or adhering to a Paleo diet, remember that even the hunter gatherers eat potatoes from time to time.

References:

de la O, V., Zazpe, I., Martínez, J. A., Santiago, S., Carlos, S., Zulet, M. Á., & Ruiz-Canela, M. (2020). Scoping review of Paleolithic dietary patterns: A definition proposal. Nutrition Research Reviews, 34(1), 78–106. https://doi.org/10.1017/s0954422420000153

Hardy, K., Bocherens, H., Miller, J. B., & Copeland, L. (2022). Reconstructing neanderthal diet: The case for carbohydrates. Journal of Human Evolution, 162, 103105. https://doi.org/10.1016/j.jhevol.2021.103105

Jönsson, T., Ahrén, B., Pacini, G., Sundler, F., Wierup, N., Steen, S., Sjöberg, T., Ugander, M., Frostegård, J., Göransson, L., & Lindeberg, S. (2006). A paleolithic diet confers higher insulin sensitivity, lower C-reactive protein and lower blood pressure than a cereal-based diet in domestic pigs. Nutrition & Metabolism, 3(1). https://doi.org/10.1186/1743-7075-3-39

Mårtensson, A., Stomby, A., Tellström, A., Ryberg, M., Waling, M., & Otten, J. (2021). Using a paleo ratio to assess adherence to paleolithic dietary recommendations in a randomized controlled trial of individuals with type 2 diabetes. Nutrients, 13(3), 969. https://doi.org/10.3390/nu13030969

Monterrosa, E. C., Frongillo, E. A., Drewnowski, A., de Pee, S., & Vandevijvere, S. (2020). Sociocultural influences on food choices and implications for sustainable healthy diets. Food and Nutrition Bulletin, 41(2_suppl). https://doi.org/10.1177/0379572120975874

Pontzer, H., & Wood, B. M. (2021). Effects of evolution, ecology, and economy on human diet: Insights from hunter-gatherers and other small-scale societies. Annual Review of Nutrition, 41(1), 363–385. https://doi.org/10.1146/annurev-nutr-111120-105520

Rampelli, S., Turroni, S., Mallol, C., Hernandez, C., Galván, B., Sistiaga, A., Biagi, E., Astolfi, A., Brigidi, P., Benazzi, S., Lewis, C. M., Warinner, C., Hofman, C. A., Schnorr, S. L., & Candela, M. (2021). Components of a Neanderthal gut microbiome recovered from fecal sediments from El Salt. Communications Biology, 4(1). https://doi.org/10.1038/s42003-021-01689-y

Rydhög, B., Carrera-Bastos, P., Granfeldt, Y., Sundquist, K., Sonestedt, E., Nilsson, P. M., & Jönsson, T. (2023). Inverse association between paleolithic diet fraction and mortality and incidence of cardiometabolic disease in the prospective Malmö diet and cancer study. European Journal of Nutrition, 63(2), 501–512. https://doi.org/10.1007/s00394-023-03279-6

Sohouli, M. H., Baniasadi, M., Hernández-Ruiz, Á., Magalhães, E. I., Santos, H. O., Akbari, A., & Zarrati, M. (2022). Associations of the paleolithic diet pattern scores and the risk of breast cancer among adults: A case–control study. Nutrition and Cancer, 75(1), 256–264. https://doi.org/10.1080/01635581.2022.2108466

Xiao, Y., Wang, Y., Gu, H., Xu, Z., Tang, Y., He, H., Peng, L., & Xiang, L. (2023). Adherence to the paleolithic diet and paleolithic-like lifestyle reduce the risk of colorectal cancer in the United States: A prospective cohort study. Journal of Translational Medicine, 21(1). https://doi.org/10.1186/s12967-023-04352-8

Genetics

Anais Marie Orantez

Do I look like you?
I wonder if we have the same colored hair

Or if your eyes match mine

Maybe it could be looking at a mirror reflection
A younger version

of yourself

An older version
of myself

I wonder

if mom sees you in me
I wonder

if that's why we had such a tough relationship

I wonder

how many times she's had to compose herself after realizing

She has you with her forever

And maybe

she didn't want it that way

I love when people say I look like my mom

Because every once in a while

She forgets your face

and sees mine

Genetics: Haiku

Anais Marie Orantez

Do I look like you?
Reflection or a stranger,
Mom knows, but speaks none.

Hateful Winter

Laisha Vargas Garcia

I think back to that winter night. For the past four years I have hated winter. It always reminds me of the worst time of my life. As I try to ignore this seasonal depression, I sink deeper into it—like quicksand. I shiver, at the thought of that conversation. Words that are forever engraved in my brain. The feeling of isolation as the sun goes down.

Soon, I am gasping for air just as I was that night. I feel the tears streaming down my hot cheeks; just as they once did, but you wouldn't get this. You don't have a care in the world for me. You came like a hurricane whose sole purpose was to destroy.

It has been four years, and I still hate winter. I hate the memories. I wish it would let me go. I wish these memories could be locked away forever, but alas, every year, the skies turn grey, the leaves fall off the trees, the roads icy, and my heart cold. Every winter comes back to haunt me.

Drowning

Laisha Vargas Garcia

As I swim to the surface of this ocean,
I feel electrifying strings,
pulling me down.

The faster I swim,
The deeper I sink.
Struggling.

I manage to break free,
But your tentacles have forever
Left their mark on me.

Diferentes Caminos

Esteban Moctezuma Bernal

Tú tanto estás cambiando
Y nuestro amor se va contigo
Nunca pensé perder
Lo que juramos proteger

Ya no te reconozco,
Ni el amor que tú me brindas
Parece que te alejas
Aún más lejos de mi vida

Y te encontré coraje
Con tus nuevas acciones
Y no eres la culpable
De ignorar mis emociones

Lo que pasó ayer,
Hoy se terminó
Lejos de mi, se fue tu corazón

Hoy te dejo ir,
Y tú sabes no es por mi
Y creo que es lo mejor
Desconectar el corazón
Decirnos hoy adiós
Hoy te dejo ir mi amor

Es bueno que te fijes
En tu propio destino
Pensar en ti misma
Y dejarme aquí solito

Y no te pongas triste
Son cosas de la vida
Cambiar lo que un día eres
Para encontrar tu alegría

Tal vez en un día lejano
Te encuentre en el camino
Y al ser nuevas personas
Me entregues tu cariño

Lo que pasó ayer

Hoy se terminó

Lejos de mi se fue tu corazón

Hoy te dejo ir

Y tú sabes no es por mi

Y creo que es lo mejor

Seguir al corazón

Decirnos hoy adiós

Hoy te dejo ir mi amor

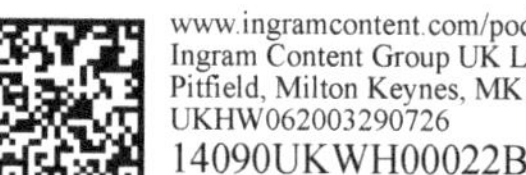

www.ingramcontent.com/pod-product-compliance
Ingram Content Group UK Ltd.
Pitfield, Milton Keynes, MK11 3LW, UK
UKHW062003290726
14090UKWH00022B/1357